PASTA IN A PINCH

CITRUSY FENNEL SALAD, page 134

PASTA IN A PINCH

Classic and Creative Recipes
Made with Everyday Pantry Ingredients

FRANCESCA MONTILLO

PHOTOGRAPHY BY
TARA DONNE

ROCKRIDGE
PRESS

For general information on our other products and services or to obtain technical support, please contact our Customer Care Department within the United States at (866) 744-2665, or outside the United States at (510) 253-0500.

Rockridge Press publishes its books in a variety of electronic and print formats. Some content that appears in print may not be available in electronic books, and vice versa.

TRADEMARKS: Rockridge Press and the Rockridge Press logo are trademarks or registered trademarks of Callisto Media Inc. and/or its affiliates, in the United States and other countries, and may not be used without written permission. All other trademarks are the property of their respective owners. Rockridge Press is not associated with any product or vendor mentioned in this book.

Interior & Cover Designer: Heather Krakora
Art Producer: Sara Feinstein
Editor: Ada Fung
Production Editor: Matt Burnett

Photography © 2020 Tara Donne. Food styling by Cyd McDowell. Illustrations used under license from iStock.com.
Author photograph courtesy of Wicked Shots Photography.

Cover (clockwise, from upper right): Gnocchi with Mozzarella, page 61; Pasta with Zucchini Pesto and Prawns, page 83; Classic Pasta Primavera, page 55; Antipasto Pasta Salad, page 98; Lemony Angel Hair, page 39.

ISBN: Print 978-1-64739-703-6 | eBook 978-1-64739-704-3

R0

To my pasta-loving dad,
Giovanni Montillo

CONTENTS

INTRODUCTION

"*Hai buttato la pasta*?" I heard that timeless question frequently while growing up in Italy. To an Italian, a day without pasta is unheard of. My dad would gaze at my mom with a look of eagerness, asking about the status of his beloved dish. Loosely translated, the question asks whether one has "thrown in the pasta"—meaning, have you added the pasta to the water yet.

I was born in southern Italy, where dried pasta is the norm. Unlike in the north, where stuffed pastas, such as tortellini, or fresh egg tagliatelle are eaten regularly, in southern Italy, store-bought dried pasta is eaten daily and prepared in countless inventive ways. It's our version of comfort food and it never disappoints, even when simply prepared with some *cacio e pepe*—grated cheese and black pepper. It was what bonded my father and me. He had a particular love for pasta and he passed that fondness on to me.

Of all the ingredients available to cook with, there isn't one as versatile as pasta. It can be served in rich and elaborate ways worthy of a fancy wedding meal, or simply prepared with everyday pantry ingredients. Picture yourself on a Friday night—you haven't gone food shopping in several weeks, but you open the cupboard and find a few ingredients that, when combined with boxed pasta, can make a delicious meal.

Pasta is achievable for the trained chef and the novice cook alike. But if you're currently holding this book, you're likely in a bit of a pasta rut. Perhaps you eat pasta regularly but prepare it in the same few ways. This book will help you emerge from that rut and discover that, when it comes to preparing pasta, you're only as limited as your imagination. In this book, you will find recipes easy enough for that Friday night, but also worthy of that dinner party you've been meaning to host but haven't yet built the culinary confidence to do so.

Unlike my previous cookbook, *The 5-Ingredient Italian Cookbook*, which was filled with traditional and regional Italian recipes, this book is a combination of those traditional pastas, as well as recipes featuring ingredients that work well together. And with our added "Another Pastability" ideas offered with many recipes, you'll see that just by changing one or two ingredients you can transform a given recipe into a completely different dish.

So, get ready to expand your pasta repertoire, gain confidence behind the stove, and master the art of preparing countless delicious pasta dishes!

CHAPTER ONE

EASY PASTA, ANY DAY OF THE WEEK

As a native Italian, I am often asked if I cook every night. Most people assume I cook every day, and they would be right! But cooking for me is never about complexity and long lists of steps and ingredients; instead, it's about ease, comfort, and creating something special from a few simple ingredients. Pasta is just that. When it comes to cooking pasta, many say it's as easy as boiling water. Although admittedly, it takes a few more steps than that, it's not *much* more work. In this book, I'll show you why pasta is the perfect weeknight meal. But before we dive into the actual recipes, I want to offer some guidance on buying and cooking pasta, the benefits of sauces, essential tools for the job, and items to stock in your fridge and pantry for effortless preparation.

PASTA, THE PERFECT WEEKNIGHT MEAL

Quick enough for any busy weeknight dinner, but versatile enough for a fancy gathering, pasta is the perfect meal for just about any occasion. You might gather with friends over a bowl of Bucatini all'Amatriciana (page 44), a sauce made with tomatoes, *guanciale* (an Italian meat product), and onion. Or you might seek comfort with a hearty dish of pasta and beans (Pasta e Fagioli, page 48). Pasta is economical, effortless, and beloved by just about everyone—a reason it's the perfect family option. A few of Italy's favorite pastas include cheese and black pepper (Cacio e Pepe, page 28), pasta with tomato sauce (Pasta al Pomodoro, page 25), and a sauce of tomatoes, anchovies, olives, capers, and garlic (Bucatini alla Puttanesca; page 30). These pantry pastas use mostly shelf-stable ingredients and a few fresh ingredients you probably already have on hand, and are ideal for those times when you need to whip up something quick, or your cupboards are looking bare.

ALL YOU NEED IS PASTA, SAUCE, AND SOMETHING ON TOP

A great pasta dish comes down to the pasta shape you select, the sauce, and whether you want a little something extra on top.

Throughout the recipes in this book, you will find pasta shape suggestions, but don't let the proposed shape dictate your meal; these are merely suggestions, and although some shapes work better with some sauces, change and swap them as desired. That's part of pasta's beauty!

Sauces are great accompaniments and can be an equal star to your pasta dish. In fact, pasta and sauces go hand in hand, and one would be lost without the other. But balance is key when cooking pasta—you don't want to drown your pasta in sauce.

Toppings, on the other hand, are generally optional but can add a little something extra, such as taste, texture, and visual appeal, to an already fabulous dish. However, don't abandon the dish if you don't have them on hand; chances are, the final dish will still be wonderful.

A word about grated cheeses: As you go through the recipes, you'll find many that call for grated cheese of one kind or another—pasta and grated cheese make an ideal marriage. In some cases, the cheese is listed as optional; in others, it's a core component of the recipe and should not be omitted. We'll explore these components and how they complement each other in the pages to come.

THE LONG AND SHORT OF PASTA SHAPES

Although the actual taste of plain boiled pasta doesn't vary much from shape to shape, the shape you select determines if and how the sauce or topping will stick to it, and whether you're better off using a spoon or fork to dig in. With hundreds of sizes and shapes, how do you choose? Most pasta shapes, with the exception of a few, are interchangeable, but this quick guide will help you determine the best match for your sauce.

Long and Lean

Time to get out the fork, and for some also a spoon, and start twirling! Long, lean pasta shapes include angel hair, bucatini, fettuccini, linguini (the most popular spaghetti), tagliatelle, thin spaghetti, vermicelli, and lesser-recognized (at least in the United States) varieties such as bigoli, capellini, and *spaghetti alla ghitarra*. Long and lean pastas work well with lighter, simpler sauces, light condiments, and seafood dishes. Most major brands have a large selection of these pasta types, so they are easy to find, and most interchange well.

The most popular question I am asked when it comes to long and lean pasta is, "Should the pasta be broken in half?" Italians do not break long pasta in half. Ever. It's placed in a large pot of salted boiling water, then gently pushed into the water fully as it softens. When it comes to eating, some require the assistance of a spoon when twirling it; some do not. Either way, there is no shaming, and it's polite to include the spoon at the table in case a guest requires it.

Long and Wide

Dry lasagna sheets have come a long way, and the newer "no-boil" noodles have changed the way we cook. This new version of lasagna sheets has made it much easier to prepare lasagna during the week, and it's the only type I use now. My preferred brand is Barilla, but there are a few other varieties out there. Other long, wide shapes include mafalde, pappardelle, and tagliatelle. These are used for heavier sauces. So, for long and wide pasta, think meat sauces and sauces with chunky vegetables in them.

Short and Tubular

Short and tubular is my all-time favorite pasta shape—the one I use the most—and the shape I find most interchangeable. It's adaptable, going well with all kinds of sauces, toppings, and meats. It's also my shape of choice for baked pasta dishes. When discussing short and tubular, I mean the most popular and easy-to-find penne rigate, (lined penne), penne lisce (smooth penne), ziti, rigatoni, and mezzi rigatoni (half the length of regular rigatoni). Garganelli, mostaccioli, and paccheri are also in the same genre but a bit more difficult to find. All of these shapes are great options for many sauces and toppings in this book. When you see a recipe in this book specifically calling for one of these cuts, it's simply to give you an idea of the most common shape used; feel free to change it to a different shape in the same family.

A word on "macaroni," also known as elbow macaroni: Because this shape doesn't interchange well with other shapes in this category, and because it's mostly used in soups or with legumes, I have classified elbow macaroni as "teeny tiny pasta" (see page 6 for best uses for this pasta).

Short and Funky

Campanelle, cavatappi, farfalle, fusilli, gemelli, medium shells, orecchiette, radiatori, rotini, and trofie are just a few varieties of somewhat oddly shaped pastas ideal for recipes that are fun, light, and downright entertaining. I most often use these shapes for pasta salads, dishes using chunky vegetables, or other thick and chunky sauces or toppings. Recipes calling for these shapes typically call for the use of a fork as opposed to a spoon to eat. Fusilli and farfalle (butterflies) are perhaps the most famous shapes and easily found from manufacturers such as Barilla and Prince. Orecchiette are frequently paired with broccoli rabe and sausage to make a famous dish from the Puglia region of Italy. The name orecchiette means "little ears," for that is what they resemble. Fusilli looks like a twisted corkscrew, and its shape makes it the ideal vessel for sauce to stick to. Trofie is a short, thin, twisted specialty of the Veneto region, and it's usually used in basil pesto dishes along with other sauces. Campanelle means "little bells" in Italian and, as the name implies, they look like flower-shaped bells. These pasta varieties are wonderful in recipes utilizing thick sauces because their curved shapes catch and hold the sauce.

Teeny Tiny Pasta

Teeny tiny pasta comes in many varieties, the most popular of which are ditalini, elbows, mini farfalle, orzo, small shells, and the super-tiny pastina and acini di pepe. Fregola is also a famous tiny pasta option, which looks like tiny balls and comes from the Italian region of Sardinia. Orzo resembles flattened rice kernels and it's one of my favorites to have on hand. Tiny pasta is perfect for adding to soups and stews or mixing with small vegetables such as peas, and with legumes such as cannellini beans, chickpeas, and lentils. This cut of pasta is generally best served with a spoon. It cooks quickly, is favored by kids and adults alike, and makes an excellent addition to your pantry. Barilla, Prince, and Ronzoni, as well as store brands, offer countless options for tiny pasta.

GET SAUCY

Sauce, pasta's most beloved partner, is as important as the shape you select. When we use the term "sauce," many people immediately picture the red kind, but we're talking far beyond red sauce here. Sauce encompasses the creaminess of a delicious Alfredo, a garlicky clam sauce, and a zingy lemon sauce, to name just a few. Read on for some guidance on how to best prepare your sauce.

Save Your Pasta Cooking Water

The importance of the pasta water can't be overstated. Chefs call it "liquid gold" and consider it a culinary crime to toss that liquid down the drain. Why? After all, to the eye, it looks cloudy, and one might even say dirty, but that's because it's full of flavor from the starch and salt. The starch in pasta water helps thicken your sauces, giving the finished dish a silky texture. The water itself acts as an emulsifier—when water is added to fat, such as olive oil, butter, or cream, it creates a creamy, but not greasy, sauce. This salty, starchy goodness is a key difference between perfectly good pasta and blow-your-mind delicious restaurant-quality pasta. When you add pasta water to a sauce, start small and add a few tablespoons at a time. Though the water will thin out the sauce at first, the sauce eventually thickens as the starch is absorbed.

ALTERNATIVE PASTAS

No matter the diet you adhere to, when it comes to traditional refined pasta alternatives, we're not lacking for choices these days. A number of recipes in this book can easily be modified to use one of the following options:

Brown rice: Brown rice pasta has more fiber than traditional pasta, is sturdier, and has a stronger texture. As a result, it works best with thick, chunky, meaty sauces as opposed to light sauces. It generally takes longer to cook than traditional pasta, so test for doneness while cooking.

Chickpea: Pasta made with chickpea flour is naturally gluten free, loaded with protein and fiber, and contains fewer carbs than traditional pasta. It cooks in less time than traditional pasta, with al dente doneness reached within 5 to 7 minutes. Popular brands include Banza, Barilla, and a few store brands, such as Wegmans.

Gluten free: The texture of gluten-free pasta varies a bit from the traditional variety, but aside from that, it is easily interchangeable with other pastas. Cooking times vary, so check the box for accurate cooking instructions. Some other gluten-free options include brown rice, chickpea, and quinoa pasta.

Whole wheat: Whole-wheat pasta packs more nutrients, more fiber, and fewer calories than traditional pasta. It's also less processed and contains more of the wheat's bran and germ. Because of that, you'll need a few more minutes of cooking time. Whole-wheat pasta can easily be swapped in, but because of its denser texture, it works best with thick, robust meat or vegetable sauces. Many major brands and store brands offer whole-wheat options.

Spiralized vegetables: Thanks to the invention of the spiralizer, many people now spiralize vegetables and use them in place of pasta. These obviously aren't pastas; they are simply vegetables shaped to look like long pasta. Still, these can be a fun, healthy alternative and an interesting way to eat fewer carbs, or to get a picky child to eat more vegetables. They work best with very light sauces and recipes that call for spaghetti or other long, thin pasta. Most spiralized veggies cook in far less time than traditional pasta.

The Sauce-to-Pasta Ratio

Sauces and toppings are great, but it's important to strike a balance. The pasta should be tossed in the sauce, not overpowered by it. A little bit of leftover sauce is nice so you can mop it up with a nice piece of crusty bread, but not an entire loaf! For red sauces, I recommend about 3 cups of sauce per 1 pound of pasta. For pestos, much less is needed—closer to just 1 cup. For other less creamy sauces, just enough to coat, not overpower, the pasta will do. And it's always best to add the pasta to the sauce, not the other way around. Pasta that has finished its cooking in the sauce tastes completely different from boiled pasta to which sauce has been added. (I'm convinced this is one of every Italian home cook's best-kept secrets!)

Ingredient Balance Is Key

I believe Italian cooking, in general, places a strong emphasis on highlighting the simple beauty of quality ingredients and how delicious just a few complementary ingredients can be. For example, many seafood pasta dishes do wonderfully with just some garlic, fresh parsley, lemon, and great olive oil. Pesto is just a handful of high quality fresh ingredients blended together.

So, don't be tempted to go overboard with ingredients under the assumption that by adding on, you're adding flavor; in fact, you could be on your way to "too much." Many busy moms in Italy turn to the staple *pasta al burro e Parmigiano*, or well-cooked pasta with high quality butter and Parmesan cheese, for their little eaters. And although your tastes may be more refined and require more flavor, most people find they don't need *that* much more.

Let the Flavor Build

Building flavor in your recipes isn't complicated or mysterious, especially when you start with great ingredients; and building flavor is never about adding extra ingredients, but about pulling as much flavor as possible from the ones you're using. Here's a short list on how to add flavor to sauces, each of which takes just a few minutes or a few minor alterations to ingredients:

Add herbs. Dried herbs are a wonderful addition to many dishes. Rub them between your fingers to release their natural oils before adding them to a recipe. If time permits, toast them in a small skillet before using for added flavor. Keep the heat low and stir consistently so they don't burn. Fresh herbs are also wonderful flavor enhancers. Add them to sauces while cooking or at the end for both garnish and flavor.

Deglaze the pan. Don't dismiss all those browned bits on the bottom of the pan as burnt food. Those bits are loaded with flavor! Deglaze your pan by adding a few tablespoons of liquid, such as pasta water, wine, or stock. Then turn up the heat and, using a wooden spoon, scrape up all those bits and pour the thickened sauce over the pasta.

Reduce the sauce. Reducing sauce concentrates the flavors further and enhances all the ingredients. The best ways to reduce sauces include adding just a bit of starchy pasta water, letting the liquid evaporate by keeping the lid off while cooking, and increasing the heat.

Remove water from veggies. The most efficient way to enhance and build flavor in vegetables is to remove as much of their natural liquid as possible. That's why boiled vegetables can be bland—but take the same vegetables, cook them in a skillet with a little olive oil, onion, and garlic, and they take on an entirely new flavor.

Season liberally with salt. Seems straightforward, right? Salt pulls the moisture from vegetables and meats. Because water has no flavor, the less of it contained in your ingredients and finished dish, the more flavor you'll have. Salt makes bitter foods more palatable and sweet foods sweeter.

TOP IT! THE CRUNCHY, CHEESY, ZINGY BITS

If you're feeling creative or have the urge to add a little something distinct to your final dish, toppings are a smart way to go. Although toppings aren't the most significant part of the recipe, they are a great way to enhance your plate. Consider:

Extra-virgin olive oil (EVOO). Topping a dish with a drizzle of peppery olive oil gives it a glistening visual appeal, improved taste, and more substance. EVOO is a safe bet to top just about any recipe. For cooking, it's fine to use the less expensive, regular olive oil.

Fresh herbs. Fresh flat-leaf parsley and basil are Italy's most preferred fresh herbs, used both for garnish and to add freshness to a finished dish. Herbs are the difference-makers in pasta recipes featuring chicken, turkey, and seafood. Thyme and sage are also widely used.

Grated cheese. Be it Parmesan, Pecorino Romano, or other hard cheeses, grated cheese is, by far, the most prolific topping used on pasta dishes. It adds lots of flavor, saltiness, and zest. Few are the pasta dishes in Italy not topped with some form of grated cheese. Avoid pregrated, shelf-stable cheese, which has been shown to contain fillers. Instead, buy large chunks and grate as needed.

Lemon zest. Lemon zest makes a wonderfully bright topping for seafood pasta dishes, pasta salads, or other light sauces. But use sparingly—you don't want to overpower the dish, and, generally, avoid using lemon with red sauces as the combination is very acidic.

Nuts. Walnuts, pecans, hazelnuts, and pine nuts are some favorite pasta toppings for many reasons. They add protein and crunch and can make a simple dish a bit more elegant. They work best with vegetarian dishes that lack other proteins.

Soft cheese. Shredded mozzarella, a spoonful of ricotta, or shavings of ricotta salata all have the ability to elevate even the simplest dishes. These cheeses work best with red sauces, meat sauces, baked pastas, and recipes without seafood. I always use whole-milk mozzarella, which tastes better and is less rubbery, and whole-milk ricotta, which is less watery than its part-skim or low-fat counterparts.

Toasted bread crumbs. In olden days, when cheeses were less affordable, it was common for pasta to be topped with toasted bread crumbs. They served as a cheap "mock cheese." And although grated cheeses in varying price points are now available, topping a dish with toasted bread crumbs still adds good crunch and flavor. Toast them for a few minutes in a pan beforehand so they will better soak up whatever sauce you are using.

THE FORMULA FOR A QUICK PANTRY PASTA

Here's a quick formula for how to put together a pantry pasta that uses mostly shelf-stable ingredients and/or a few fresh ones you probably have on hand.

COOK THE PASTA

large pot + 4 quarts water + 1½-2 tbsp salt

cover + boil
+
pasta

stir + cook until al dente

MAKE THE SAUCE

large skillet + 2-3 tbsp olive oil
(more for oil-based sauces)
+
aromatics
e.g. garlic, onion, red pepper flakes
+
sauce ingredients
bacon + canned white beans OR
canned tuna + capers OR
anchovies + capers OR
marinated artichokes +
sun-dried tomatoes

If making a tomato sauce, add crushed tomatoes and simmer uncovered

stir + cook until ingredients are done and married together

REMOVE PASTA + ADD TO SAUCE
stir to coat evenly

Add ladleful of pasta water to thicken sauce

Top it!
e.g. fresh parsley, grated Parmesan or Romano, drizzle of EVOO

10 TIPS FOR MAKING PASTA

From water amounts to salting the water, read on for some tried-and-true tips for optimizing your pasta cooking efforts.

1. **Use plenty of water.** Many home cooks underestimate the amount of water needed when it comes to boiling pasta. We may be tempted to use too small a pot or too little water, but pasta expands and releases a lot of starch when cooking, so the pot must be big and the water ample. As a rule, use at least 4 quarts of water (1 gallon) in a 6-quart pot for every 1 pound of pasta, and cook the pasta uncovered to prevent overflow.

2. **Salt liberally.** Pasta water should taste like seawater! For every 1 pound of pasta, aim for at least 1 tablespoon of table salt. Some people use up to 2 tablespoons. Try the same recipe using varying amounts of salt and see what you prefer. Keep in mind that this is the only chance you'll have to season the actual pasta without the added sauce or condiment. You can use table salt, iodized or not, but iodized salt can leave behind a metallic aftertaste.

3. **Wait for a rolling boil.** A watched pot never boils, or so the saying goes. But don't let this tempt you into adding the pasta to the water too early. The pasta should be added to the water once it comes to a full rolling boil, or it might turn sticky, clumpy, and gummy. Either way, it will take just as long to come to the al dente stage, so wait for that good boil.

4. **Cook to al dente.** Use the instructions on the box as a general guide, not a rule. Italians prefer their pasta al dente, or to the tooth, meaning it still has some bite. Generally, instructions given on pasta boxes cook it past the point of al dente; so, if the box says to cook for 10 minutes, start tasting at the 8-minute mark. For pasta bakes and dishes finished in the oven, stop the stovetop cooking at the halfway mark, as the pasta will continue cooking in the oven. If you're finishing your dish in the sauce, as many recipes in this book do, cook for 1 to 2 minutes less than al dente.

5. **Stir frequently.** The pasta is most likely to stick together into one giant clump within the first few minutes of being added to the water; that's

when it releases the most starch. So, stir often during those first few minutes. After that, you can back off a bit, but don't go too far—it's still important to stir frequently.

6. **Save your oil.** As a culinary instructor, I am often asked by my students whether to add oil to the cooking water. The answer is no. There is no good reason for adding it; in fact, it will turn your pasta oily and make it difficult for your sauce to stick to the pasta. Save the oil for the sauce or add it at the end as a finisher.

7. **Taste test.** The difference between undercooked, al dente, and mushy pasta is just a few minutes. That's why it's important to go by taste and not what the box says for cooking times. The only way to tell if the pasta is done is by tasting it, so don't be shy—grab a strand, a few noodles, a penne or two, and bite into it.

8. **Save some pasta water.** Pasta water contains lots of flavor and starches, so reserve some in case you need it. The starch works as a thickening agent. So, if your sauce is a bit on the thin side, adding a few tablespoons of pasta water will help thicken it.

9. **Strain right away.** Once cooked, immediately remove the pasta from the water. Letting the pasta sit in the water, even with the heat off, continues its cooking process and results in mushy pasta.

10. **Skip the rinse!** There's no reason to rinse pasta after it's cooked. Rinsing washes away all the starch, flavor, and saltiness. If you're preparing a pasta salad, add all the ingredients and let it come to room temperature once combined. If you must combine everything later, add 1 to 2 teaspoons of oil to the cooked pasta to prevent clumping.

STOCKING YOUR PASTA KITCHEN

All the recipes in this book are only as good as the ingredients used to create them—that means having a well-stocked pantry, fridge, and freezer is key. Not only will the final product be that much more delicious, it will save time in the long run. No one likes realizing mid prep that they're missing that one ingredient! Following is an essential list of ingredients for the pastas in this book as well as hundreds of other Italian recipes.

In the Pantry

Canned anchovies. A staple ingredient, especially in southern Italian cuisine, anchovies add lots of flavor for very little cost. A must-have ingredient in puttanesca sauce (Bucatini alla Puttanesca, page 30), anchovies are also an excellent addition to Aglio, Olio, e Peperoncino (page 24).

Canned crushed tomatoes. Canned crushed tomatoes are an excellent starting point for many recipes. Try a few varieties until you find one you love. Some of my favorite brands include Cento, Muir Glen, Pastene, and Tutto Rosso. I also love the more expensive, but worth it, San Marzano, a variety of tomato sold under several brands.

Canned and dried beans and legumes. Although I love the flavor and sturdiness of dried legumes, they need to be soaked before cooking and that requires some planning. Canned is a wonderful alternative for soups and in Pasta e Fagioli (page 48). I always rinse and drain canned legumes before using to reduce their sodium.

Canned tuna. I prefer the Italian tuna packed in extra-virgin olive oil. It's readily available in chain supermarkets and adds flavor incomparable to the one packed in water. Genova and Pastene are high quality brands.

Capers. Salt-cured capers find their way into many Sicilian dishes and offer a lot of flavor and saltiness to a dish. Watch the added salt when using capers, as they are salty to start. Rinse them before adding to your recipe.

Dried herbs and red pepper flakes. A few of my favorite dried herbs include bay leaves, oregano, rosemary, and thyme. Rub them between your fingers to extract their natural oils before adding to your recipe. Red pepper flakes are often used in southern Italian dishes, which are generally spicier than dishes from the north.

Nuts. Nuts add a great crunch to any pasta dish; a few of my favorites to add to savory dishes include pine nuts and walnuts. Pine nuts are especially great to keep on hand for various pestos.

Olive oils. Extra-virgin olive oil is best used to finish a dish; it's tastiest when eaten raw and it's worth the higher price tag it brings. But because much of the robust flavor of EVOO is lost during the cooking process, regular and less expensive olive oils will work just fine for cooking.

Rice. Although this book is mainly focused on pasta, rice is a wonderful alternative to any recipe calling for orzo or other small-cut pasta.

Salt. Salt is a must when boiling pasta. Boiling pasta in unsalted water results in a bland, unflavored dish. My recipes use regular table salt, unless otherwise directed.

Tomato paste. This pantry staple adds depth and body to sauces, soups, and stews. A little goes a long way, so a container should last you a while. Once opened, canned tomato paste will last about a week in the fridge. Tomato paste that comes in a glass jar will last a bit longer, 7 to 10 days, refrigerated. You get even more longevity from a tube, which will last up to 45 days in the fridge.

Various pasta shapes. Stock up and build a collection of varying pastas to use.

On the Counter

Garlic. It's not merely a stereotype that Italians use a lot of garlic! Found in many dishes, especially seafood, garlic is a must in your kitchen. Garlic will keep up to several months, but it should be stored in a dark, dry place with good air circulation to prevent spoiling.

Onions. Soups and many sauces would be bland without onions. I love the sweetness delivered by red onions, but traditional white or yellow onions easily substitute in any recipe. Store onions in a cool, ventilated place. If using just half an onion, refrigerate the other half and use it within a few days.

Potatoes. Italians eat a lot of potatoes in soups, stews, and, yes, even pasta. A homey comfort food, pasta and potatoes, such as Grandma's Cavatelli with Potatoes (page 57) is common in Italy, especially in cold winter months.

In the Fridge and Freezer

Bread crumbs. Although you could store bread crumbs in the cupboard, I find they last longer in the fridge. Use homemade bread crumbs whenever possible, or the bakery ones, as they are fresher than those on the store shelf.

Cheese. From melty cheeses, such as sliced mozzarella and provolone, to dry ones for grating, such as Parmesan and Romano, to soft ricotta, you'll want a few varieties of cheeses in your fridge.

Cured meats. Ham, prosciutto, salami, and soppressata are my favored Italian deli meats. But only purchase them as needed—once sliced at the deli counter, they immediately start to lose freshness. Although freshly sliced is best, if you want to plan ahead, purchase these items in vacuum-sealed containers as they last substantially longer (unopened) than the cured meats you get at the deli counter.

Eggs. Spaghetti alla Carbonara (page 43), well, just wouldn't be carbonara without fresh eggs. Eggs are also used in many baked pasta dishes.

Fresh herbs. You will always find fresh flat-leaf parsley in my fridge—I would be lost without this staple. When it's in season, I also have lots of basil, both in the fridge and in a vase on my windowsill. Other fresh herbs I love for pasta dishes include rosemary, sage, and thyme.

Fresh vegetables. Some favorites include bell peppers, broccoli, chard, eggplant, green beans, peas, spinach, and zucchini. Try to buy in-season produce as much as possible (it's tastier and usually less expensive), and always select produce free of any noticeable blemishes or brown spots.

Frozen vegetables. Frozen vegetables have come a long way and are a wonderful alternative to their fresh counterparts. Some of my favorites include broccoli florets, mixed vegetables for soups, and spinach. But my all-time can't-do-without-it frozen veggie is peas—you will find peas featured in a number of recipes in this book.

Half-and-half or heavy (whipping) cream. You may be surprised to see cream listed in a pasta book, but in Italy, we have an ingredient called *panna di cucina*—it's a lighter cream used regularly in preparing creamy sauces. Try a few recipes in this book that call for added cream and you might soon be addicted, too.

Lemons. Rare is a day in my kitchen when you can't find lemons. Lemons are the best accompaniment for seafood dishes, and for my Lemony Angel Hair (page 39). Fresh lemons can keep in the crisper for up to a month.

Meats. Thin chicken breasts, chicken tenders, boneless chicken thighs, turkey cutlets, ground beef, ground turkey, and various cuts of beef are generally found in my freezer. Boneless meats defrost and cook faster and are that much more convenient for weeknight preparation.

Sausages. Sausages are wonderful additions to countless recipes and Italians love cooking with them. One alternative to fresh sausages that I love and always keep in the fridge is fully cooked chicken sausages. They're great simply fried on the stovetop with some oil, bell pepper, and onion, and they make a great topping for pasta and pasta salads.

JUST FREEZE IT

We live in hurried times, so make your freezer your friend. With a little planning on weekends when you have more time, you've got dinner in no time on weekdays when dinner needs to be on the table in a hurry. Here's how to enlist your freezer to help:

Freeze in-season herbs and pesto. There's always an overabundance of fresh basil in the summer, but not so much in colder months, so consider making several batches of fresh basil pesto (see Pasta with Basil Pesto, page 27) and freezing it in small containers or an ice-cube tray. Fresh basil and parsley can also be frozen for use later. Simply wash the herbs under cold water, dry thoroughly with clean paper towels, and place them in small freezer bags.

Freeze pastas for another day. Any baked pasta dishes in this book, such as the Classic Pasta al Forno (page 128), Easier Weeknight Lasagna (page 123), and Baked Pasta with Ground Beef and Mozzarella (page 125), will freeze nicely. Prepare the dish up to the point that the recipe instructs to place it in the oven. Instead, at that point, wrap it in a layer of aluminum foil followed by plastic wrap for extra insurance against freezer burn. Place it in the freezer and bake it when you need it. Thaw completely in the refrigerator overnight the day before baking. Unwrap and bake according to the recipe instructions.

Also worth adding to your freezer are heartier pastas and pasta soups like Penne alla Vodka (page 35), Pasta al Pomodoro (page 25), Pasta alla Norma (page 37), Pasta e Fagioli (page 48), and Lentil and Pasta Soup with Spinach and Sausage (page 112). Store the final dish in an airtight container and thaw before reheating. I don't recommend storing pasta for longer than 1 month.

Freeze sauces. Many sauces freeze wonderfully, and making a double batch takes little to no extra effort or time. Consider freezing several cups of tomato sauce for future use. Thawing it in the fridge before using is best, but microwaving is also acceptable.

PASTA COOKING NECESSITIES

These multi-purpose utensils will ensure easy and convenient pasta preparation:

Colander. Although pasta water has its benefits, there will be times, like cooking lasagna sheets or large shells for stuffing, when you will need to drain all the water. Colanders are also great for rinsing and straining all sorts of vegetables.

Deep baking dish. Great for baked pastas and trays of lasagna. Select one that is deep and easy to clean and that can go from the oven to fridge to store leftovers.

Good set of knives. More accidents happen in the kitchen from using dull knives than sharp ones! Grab a multi-size set that is comfortable for your hand size and shape.

Grater/zester. I use this tool mostly to grate fresh Parmesan cheese, but an inexpensive rasp-style grater can be used on citrus as well.

Ladle. Great for scooping out pasta water and adding it directly to your saucepan.

Pasta fork. A pasta fork allows you to pull long pasta out of the pot without draining all the water.

Pasta pots. Although it's recommended to use 4 quarts of water for every 1 pound of pasta, there will be times when you're cooking less, or cooking a tiny pasta that doesn't require a large pot. Buy a set with various pot sizes and use them for hundreds of recipes and for years to come.

Sauté pan or skillet and saucepans. A stockpile of assorted saucepans and skillets is invaluable for sauces and finishing pasta dishes.

Spider. Great for transferring small pasta from the water to a saucepan.

Tongs. These are great for fishing out long pastas, especially thicker ones such as fettuccini or pappardelle.

Wooden spoons. Pasta calls for a good amount of stirring, so you'll want to have a stack of assorted wooden spoons.

JAZZING UP A CAN OF TOMATOES

If there's one item you will always find in my pantry, it's canned crushed tomatoes. Because fresh vine-ripened tomatoes are only in season for a short period, it's a good idea to have several cans of this staple in your pantry. I stock up when they're on sale and use this ingredient several times a week or more. Jazzing up a can of crushed tomatoes for a quick sauce is as easy as can be, requiring just a few ingredients. My staple additions to a simple sauce include finely chopped onion, garlic, fresh parsley, and olive oil. Toss in a handful of fresh basil to add a taste of summer, if desired. To step it up further, add 8 ounces cremini mushrooms for substance and a flavor boost. You can also bump up the flavor with 1 or 2 chopped large red bell peppers, or give it a kick with red pepper flakes!

ABOUT THE RECIPES

Most recipes call for either 8 ounces or 1 pound of pasta, and most recipes serve 4 to 6 people. Of course, these are just guidelines—feel free to adjust as needed. As a rule, 1 pound of pasta will serve 4 people generously. If you are serving accompaniments such as salads or a second course, that pound of pasta will easily stretch to 6 servings. Furthermore, with simple light sauces, like cacio e pepe, 1 pound of pasta will serve 4 versus a pasta with a more robust sauce, such as a hearty ragù, which will serve 6.

Recipe Labels

Most recipes come with a label for added guidance in the kitchen:

5-ingredient. These recipes call for just 5 ingredients, not counting the water needed to boil the pasta, oil, salt, and pepper.

30 Minutes or Less. In a hurry? Look for this label for recipes that take 30 minutes or less from prep to plate!

Pantry Pasta. These recipes use shelf-stable and/or everyday fresh ingredients that you likely have on hand, like onion, garlic, lemon, milk, butter, eggs, and cheese.

Worth the Wait. Some special pasta dishes are just worth the wait. But don't be discouraged—most of these recipes require less than 30 minutes of prep and the oven does the rest of the work for you.

Another Pastability

Many recipes in this book offer a variation, or "another pastability," meaning that with just one or two minor changes, you'll have a completely different recipe! Sometimes the swap can be as simple as changing the pasta shape, the vegetable or legume, or the preparation method. Pasta is inexpensive, adaptable, and flexible to whatever you add to it, and this section will help you think outside the (pasta) box.

Recipe Tips

At the end of most recipes, you'll find a useful tip to provide prep and cooking guidance, to offer ideas for what to pair with your pasta, or to provide substitution suggestions for dietary needs.

CHAPTER TWO

THE CLASSICS

Growing up in southern Italy, I ate my share of pasta. My father was a greengrocer, and he owned a small business selling mostly produce. He would come home for lunch, as my sister and I did from school, and my mom would have a nice pasta lunch waiting for us. These recipes are classic for a reason—they're prepared by just about everyone in Italy and they're what many of us grew up on, celebrated with, and adore. They are nostalgic and sentimental, but they come together quickly and many require just a handful of ingredients. I'm sure many of these will become classics in your home.

AGLIO, OLIO, E PEPERONCINO

Serves 4 to 6

Prep time: 5 minutes / Cook time: 15 minutes

5-Ingredient / 30 Minutes or Less

This dish is a favorite peasant dish from the Campania region of Italy. The recipe calls for just a few economical ingredients that most every home cook has on hand. Often eaten in olden times, when resources were low, it's now a favorite for college students living on a budget, or for those times when you haven't been to the grocery store in a while.

Table salt

1 pound spaghetti or other long, thin pasta

¼ cup olive oil

Red pepper flakes, for seasoning

4 large garlic cloves, minced

1 tablespoon chopped fresh parsley

¼ cup grated Pecorino Romano cheese

1. In a 6-quart pot over high heat, bring 4 quarts of salted water to a boil. Add the pasta, stir, and cook for about 2 minutes less than the box instructs to just under al dente.

2. Meanwhile, as the pasta cooks, in a large sauté pan or skillet over medium heat, heat the olive oil. Add the red pepper flakes to taste and the garlic. Cook for 1 to 2 minutes, or until the garlic turns golden, paying close attention that it does not burn.

3. Reserve ¼ cup of pasta water and drain the pasta. Add the spaghetti to the skillet and toss well to coat. Add 1 or 2 tablespoons of pasta water and continue tossing for about 1 minute more until the water evaporates.

4. Remove from the heat and add the parsley and Pecorino Romano cheese. Serve hot.

ANOTHER PASTABILITY

Aglio, Olio, e Peperoncino with Rotisserie Chicken: Add some chopped store-bought rotisserie chicken in step 2, and you'll have a completely different flavor profile. The white meat works particularly well here. Try it both ways and see which you prefer.

PASTA AL POMODORO

Serves 4 to 6

Prep time: 10 minutes / **Cook time:** 30 minutes

There are as many variations of pasta al pomodoro as there are *nonnas* (grandmothers) in Italy! This simple recipe has served me well for years. Because the ingredients are so simple, quality is paramount, especially for the canned crushed tomatoes.

3 tablespoons olive oil

½ small onion, finely diced

2 tablespoons chopped fresh parsley

2 garlic cloves, finely minced

1 (28-ounce) can crushed tomatoes

1 cup water

½ teaspoon salt, plus more for the pasta water

3 to 5 fresh basil leaves

1 pound pasta of choice

Freshly grated Parmesan or Romano cheese, for serving (optional)

1. In a large sauté pan or skillet over medium heat, heat the olive oil. Add the onion and parsley. Cook for 2 to 3 minutes, stirring frequently until the onion is translucent. Add the garlic and cook, stirring, for 1 minute more.

2. Carefully add the tomatoes (they will splatter) and water, along with the salt and basil. Reduce the heat to low, cover the pan, and simmer for 20 minutes.

3. Meanwhile, in a 6-quart pot over high heat, bring 4 quarts of salted water to a boil. Add the pasta, stir, and cook for about 2 minutes less than the box instructs to just under al dente.

4. Remove 1 cup of sauce and set aside. Drain the pasta and add it to the sauce in the pan. Mix to coat evenly and cook for 1 to 2 minutes.

5. Divide the pasta among individual plates and top each with 1 or 2 tablespoons of the reserved sauce. Sprinkle with the grated cheese (if using).

Prep tip: Make extra sauce to freeze for another day! It will keep, frozen, for 2 to 3 months. Thawing overnight in the fridge is best, but in a pinch, the microwave will work.

RIGATONI WITH SPICY ARRABIATA

Serves 4 to 6

Prep time: 10 minutes / **Cook time:** 25 minutes

This is another favorite red sauce of Italy that's also served in many Italian American restaurants. Once you see how easy it is to prepare, you might never order it out again. The key is using fresh red pepper flakes. Oftentimes, the ones we have at home have been sitting in our cupboards for a while, and they lose potency as they age.

3 tablespoons olive oil

½ to 2 teaspoons red pepper flakes

½ teaspoon salt, plus more for the pasta water

2 garlic cloves, minced

2 tablespoons chopped fresh parsley

2 tablespoons tomato paste

1 (28-ounce) can crushed tomatoes

1 pound rigatoni or other pasta of choice

Grated Pecorino Romano cheese, for serving (optional)

1. In a large sauté pan or skillet over low heat, heat the olive oil. Add the pepper flakes and salt and cook for 1 to 2 minutes. Stir in the garlic and parsley and cook, stirring, for 1 minute more. Add the tomato paste and break it down, mixing well with a wooden spoon.

2. Carefully and slowly add the crushed tomatoes (they will splatter). Cover the pan and cook for 15 to 18 minutes, stirring occasionally.

3. Meanwhile, in a 6-quart pot over high heat, bring 4 quarts of salted water to a boil. Add the pasta, stir, and cook for about 2 minutes less than the box instructs to just under al dente.

4. Drain the pasta and add it to the sauce, mixing well to coat the pasta. Cook the pasta and sauce together for several minutes. Serve immediately topped with the Pecorino Romano cheese (if using).

Cooking tip: Arrabiata is defined as "angry," meaning this dish is supposed to be very spicy. That said, add the red pepper flakes in increments, tasting as you go, so you don't go too far.

PASTA WITH BASIL PESTO

Serves 4

Prep time: 5 minutes / **Cook time:** 10 minutes

5-Ingredient / 30 Minutes or Less

Pasta with pesto is a favorite summer dish hailing from the Liguria region of Italy. It's made with fresh basil, as it doesn't work well with previously frozen basil. That said, once made, pesto freezes beautifully! Make some pesto ahead and freeze it in ice-cube trays. Once frozen, remove the cubes from the tray and place them in freezer bags. One cube is about the perfect amount for one serving of pasta.

¼ teaspoon salt, plus more for the pasta water

1 pound pasta of choice

6 cups fresh basil leaves

3 garlic cloves, peeled

¼ cup extra-virgin olive oil, divided

¼ cup pine nuts

½ cup freshly grated Parmesan cheese, Pecorino Romano cheese, or a combination

1. In a 6-quart pot over high heat, bring 4 quarts of salted water to a boil. Add the pasta, stir, and cook according to the instructions on the box for al dente.

2. Meanwhile, in a food processor, combine the basil, ¼ teaspoon of salt, the garlic, and 2 tablespoons of olive oil. Pulse for 1 to 2 minutes, stopping to press down the basil leaves.

3. Add the pine nuts and the remaining 2 tablespoons of olive oil. Continue pulsing for 1 to 2 minutes more until a paste begins to form and the pine nuts are fully ground. Add the grated cheese and pulse for about 1 minute until a creamy paste forms.

4. Drain the pasta and return it to the still-warm pot. Add the pesto, mix well, and serve hot or at room temperature.

ANOTHER PASTABILITY

Pasta with other pestos: Basil pesto is classic, but did you know you can make the same recipe using other leafy greens, such as spinach, chard, or even parsley? Purple basil is also beautiful and offers a different take on this classic sauce. Follow the same steps and mix it up a bit!

CACIO E PEPE

Serves 4 to 6

Prep time: 5 minutes / **Cook time:** 15 minutes

5-Ingredient / 30 Minutes or Less / Pantry Pasta

Cacio e pepe (literally "cheese and pepper") is a classic Roman Italian dish requiring very few ingredients, but yielding a tasty, satisfying dinner. It's a minimalist dish beloved by adults, and even kids with refined palates, although if serving to youngsters, monitor the black pepper used. Jazz this up by adding a can of anchovies with oil in step 2.

Table salt

1 pound spaghetti, bucatini, or other long pasta

⅓ cup olive oil

1 tablespoon butter

¾ cup freshly grated Parmesan cheese

½ cup freshly grated Pecorino Romano cheese

1 tablespoon freshly ground black pepper

1. In a 6-quart pot over high heat, bring 4 quarts of salted water to a boil. Add the pasta, stir, and cook for about 2 minutes less than the box instructs to just under al dente.

2. Using tongs, remove the pasta from the water and transfer it to a large sauté pan or skillet over medium-low heat. Add the olive oil, butter, and ½ cup of pasta water. Bring everything to a low simmer and stir, coating the pasta with the sauce.

3. Reduce the heat to very low and stir in the Parmesan cheese. Toss everything to mix well and coat evenly.

4. Remove from the heat and add the Pecorino Romano cheese and pepper. Mix well. If the pasta is drier than you like, add 1 or 2 more tablespoons of hot pasta water. Serve immediately while hot.

Substitution tip: Grated Romano cheese adds a nice sharpness, but you can use all Parmesan. Alternatively, if you don't have Parmesan, use all Romano. The key is for whatever you use to be freshly grated and of good quality. If you go with Romano, add it after the dish is cooked—otherwise it will clump.

FETTUCCINI ALFREDO

Serves 4 to 6

Prep time: 5 minutes **/ Cooking time:** 15 minutes

5-Ingredient / 30 Minutes or Less / Pantry Pasta

Conflicting information circulates on the origin of this dish. Many say it's not at all Italian, but perhaps Italian American. Others believe it was invented in Italy by a chef named Alfredo, who owned a restaurant in Rome and named a similar dish after himself. Either way, a well-prepared Alfredo sauce is easier than you think and always a crowd-pleaser.

Table salt

1 pound fettuccini or other long pasta

4 tablespoons (½ stick) salted butter

1 cup freshly grated Parmesan cheese, plus more for topping

Freshly ground black pepper

1. In a 6-quart pot over high heat, bring 4 quarts of salted water to a boil. Add the fettuccini, stir, and cook for about 2 minutes less than the box instructs to just under al dente.

2. Meanwhile, in a large sauté pan or skillet over medium heat, melt the butter.

3. While the pasta cooks, carefully remove one ladleful of pasta water and add it to the butter. Whisk until the butter is fully melted. Slowly add the Parmesan cheese to the butter and whisk constantly until well incorporated and melted.

4. Reserve ¼ cup of pasta water, drain the pasta, and add the pasta to the pan. Toss to coat in the sauce. Cook for 2 minutes. Add 2 to 3 more tablespoons of pasta water, if desired, to thicken the sauce.

5. Top with Parmesan cheese and pepper to taste. Serve immediately while hot.

ANOTHER PASTABILITY

Creamy Fettuccini Alfredo: Whether to add cream or not is the question when it comes to Alfredo sauce. For a richer and thicker dish, add heavy (whipping) cream instead of pasta water.

BUCATINI ALLA PUTTANESCA

Serves 4 to 6

Prep time: 10 minutes / **Cook time:** 25 minutes

Pantry Pasta

I'm often asked what the word *puttanesca* means, and I blush a little in my reply. A classic Neapolitan dish, puttanesca means "prostitute-style" pasta. As with most Italian dishes, the origin and name of this dish is not certain. Some claim the name derives from the spiciness of the dish, others say it's quick and easy, whereas others claim it was a favorite dish prepared by prostitutes for their clients!

3 tablespoons olive oil

2 garlic cloves, minced

1 teaspoon red pepper flakes

3 tablespoons capers, drained and rinsed

½ cup Kalamata olives, or other brined black olives of choice, pitted and halved

6 anchovies, chopped into 4 or 5 pieces

1 (14.5-ounce) can crushed tomatoes

1 teaspoon dried oregano

Table salt

1 pound bucatini or other long, thin pasta

1. In a large sauté pan or skillet over medium heat, heat the olive oil. Add the garlic and red pepper flakes and cook for 2 to 3 minutes, stirring frequently. Add the capers and olives. Cook for 2 to 3 minutes more, stirring occasionally. Add the chopped anchovies and use a wooden spoon to break them up. They will almost dissolve completely.

2. Stir in the tomatoes and oregano. Season with salt to taste and cook for 15 minutes, uncovered.

3. Meanwhile, in a 6-quart pot over high heat, bring 4 quarts of salted water to a boil. Add the pasta, stir, and cook for about 2 minutes less than the box instructs to just under al dente.

4. Reserve 2 to 3 tablespoons of pasta water, drain the pasta, and add the pasta to the sauce. Add the reserved pasta water and cook for 2 minutes, mixing to coat the pasta well. Serve immediately while hot.

Pair it: This is a strong, pungent sauce. Select a light Riesling or white Zinfandel to go with it so the wine does not overpower the sauce.

ANOTHER PASTABILITY

Fresh Cherry Tomato Puttanesca: This sauce also works wonderfully using fresh cherry tomatoes. Substitute 2 cups halved cherry tomatoes for the canned variety. Cook the fresh tomatoes for 15 minutes, or until they pop and their juices are released.

PASTA WITH BÉCHAMEL SAUCE

Serves 4 to 6

Prep time: 5 minutes / **Cook time:** 20 minutes

30 Minutes or Less / Pantry Pasta

Béchamel is a favored sauce in northern Italy, especially in Emilia-Romagna, and it's often used in hefty dishes such as lasagna Bolognese. By itself, it makes a delicious sauce for a quick weekday dinner. It's refined enough for adults, and simple enough to satisfy even the pickiest kids. This is a great vegetarian dish, but top the pasta with fried bits of prosciutto or pancetta if you want to add some protein. Béchamel can be frozen for up to 3 months, so double up and save it for another recipe, like Zucchini Pasta Bake with Béchamel Sauce (page 70).

2 cups whole milk

3 tablespoons butter (salted or unsalted)

¼ cup all-purpose flour

½ teaspoon salt, plus more for the pasta water

Ground nutmeg, for seasoning (optional)

1 pound pasta of choice

½ cup freshly grated Parmesan cheese

1. In a small saucepan over medium-low heat, heat the milk for 3 to 4 minutes until small bubbles form around the edge.

2. Meanwhile, in a large sauté pan or skillet over medium-low heat, melt the butter. Sift the flour over the butter, and using a wire whisk, mix well until smooth. Continue cooking the flour and butter for 1 minute, making sure they do not burn or brown.

3. Increase the heat to medium and slowly pour the hot milk over the flour and butter mixture, stirring constantly. The cream will be thick at first, but will loosen up as the milk is added.

4. Add ½ teaspoon of salt and continue whisking constantly. Season with nutmeg to taste (if using). Cook for about 10 minutes after adding the milk, or until the cream coats the whisk or a wooden spoon.

5. Meanwhile, in a 6-quart pot over high heat, bring 4 quarts of salted water to a boil. Add the pasta, stir, and cook for about 2 minutes less than the box instructs to just under al dente.

6. Drain the pasta and add it to the sauce, mix well to coat evenly, and cook for about 2 minutes more, or until al dente. Remove from the heat and add the Parmesan cheese. Serve hot.

Substitution tip: Whole milk is always preferred in this dish, but if you only have 2% on hand, don't let that stop you from preparing it. It will be a bit lighter but still delicious!

ANOTHER PASTABILITY

Baked Pasta with Béchamel: Béchamel is a wonderful sauce for baked pastas. For an easy baked pasta dish, follow the recipe, but boil the pasta for just 5 or 6 minutes. Continue with the remaining steps and place the pasta in a buttered baking dish, top with shredded mozzarella, and bake in a 375°F oven for 20 to 25 minutes.

PENNE WITH RICOTTA

Serves 4 to 6

Prep time: 5 minutes / **Cook time:** 15 minutes

5-Ingredient / 30 Minutes or Less

When I was growing up in Italy, my dad would often eat pasta with ricotta. As a child, I didn't see the appeal. I loved both ricotta and pasta, but together, it left little to be desired. As I got older, I added to and tweaked his recipe, which was just the two main ingredients. I'm sure he would agree that my version is better! If you want more flavor still, add the zest of one lemon, chopped parsley, or red pepper flakes to the ricotta mixture.

Table salt

1 pound penne or other tubular pasta

1½ cups whole-milk ricotta (not part-skim or skim)

¼ cup whole-milk or heavy (whipping) cream (not part-skim or skim)

½ cup freshly grated Parmesan cheese, plus more for topping

2 tablespoons chopped fresh basil

1. In a 6-quart pot over high heat, bring 4 quarts of salted water to a boil. Add the pasta, stir, and cook according to the instructions on the box to al dente.

2. Meanwhile, as the pasta cooks, in a medium bowl, whisk the ricotta, milk, and Parmesan cheese well to combine. Add 1 or 2 tablespoons of pasta water to thin out the ricotta. Season with salt to taste.

3. Drain the pasta and return it to the hot pot. Add the ricotta mixture and mix well so all the ingredients are incorporated and the pasta is well coated. Add the basil and more salt, if needed. Plate and top with Parmesan cheese, if desired.

ANOTHER PASTABILITY

Baked Three-Cheese Penne: Make this a three-cheese pasta by adding some shredded mozzarella and a few slices of provolone cheese to the ricotta mixture! Put everything in a baking dish and place it under the broiler for a few minutes before serving.

PENNE ALLA VODKA

Serves 4 to 6

Prep time: 10 minutes / **Cook time:** 25 minutes

This classic Italian American dish is found on many restaurant menus. The students in my cooking classes are always surprised at how easy it is to prepare. One word of advice: Use only good-quality vodka that you would drink. The flavor intensifies while cooking, so don't go for the cheap stuff thinking, "It's only for cooking."

3 tablespoons olive oil

1 small onion, cut into ¼-inch dice

2 garlic cloves, minced

1 (28-ounce) can crushed tomatoes

1 teaspoon salt, plus more for the pasta water

¼ cup vodka

¼ cup heavy (whipping) cream or half-and-half

2 tablespoons chopped fresh parsley

1 tablespoon chopped fresh basil

1 pound penne or other short tubular pasta

Freshly grated Parmesan cheese, for serving (optional)

1. In a large sauté pan or skillet over medium heat, heat the olive oil. Add the onion and garlic and cook for 3 to 4 minutes, stirring constantly, until the onion is softened.

2. Carefully add the crushed tomatoes (they will splatter), salt, and vodka and mix well. Cover the pan and cook for 13 to 15 minutes, stirring occasionally, until the sauce thickens.

3. Stir in the heavy cream. Add the parsley and basil and mix well.

4. Meanwhile, in a 6-quart pot, bring 4 quarts of salted water to a boil. Add the penne, stir, and cook for about 2 minutes less than the box instructs to just under al dente.

continued

5. Reserve 2 to 3 tablespoons of pasta water and drain the pasta. Add the pasta to the sauce and mix well to coat. Cook the pasta for 2 minutes. Stir in 2 to 3 tablespoons of pasta water if you'd like a thicker sauce. The starch in the water will thicken the sauce.

6. Remove from the heat and sprinkle with the Parmesan cheese (if using). Serve immediately while hot.

Pair it: This is a rich dish, so pair it with the Arugula and Radicchio Salad (page 132) to lighten your meal.

ANOTHER PASTABILITY

Penne alla Vodka with Prosciutto: One way to kick this up several notches is to add some prosciutto. Add about ¼ cup chopped prosciutto about halfway through step 1, and enjoy a delicious, even richer alternative to this classic.

PASTA ALLA NORMA

Serves 4 to 6

Prep time: 10 minutes **/ Cook time:** 25 minutes

A famous dish from the city of Catania, in Sicily, this dish uses one of Sicily's main summer vegetables: eggplant. The dish is believed to have been created by a chef in Catania after the opera *Norma,* composed by Vincenzo Bellini.

¼ cup olive oil

1 large or 2 medium eggplants, cut into 1-inch cubes

1 teaspoon dried oregano

½ teaspoon salt, plus more for the pasta water

Freshly ground black pepper

3 garlic cloves, minced

1 (28-ounce) can crushed tomatoes

1 pound penne or other tubular pasta

1 cup fresh whole-milk ricotta

3 to 5 fresh basil leaves, chopped

1. In a large sauté pan or skillet over medium heat, heat the olive oil. Add the eggplant. Season with the oregano, salt, and pepper to taste. Cook for 5 or 6 minutes until softened. Add the garlic and tomatoes. Reduce the heat to low, cover the pan, and simmer for 15 minutes.

2. Meanwhile, in a 6-quart pot over high heat, bring 4 quarts of salted water to a boil. Add the pasta, stir, and cook for about 2 minutes less than the box instructs to just under al dente.

3. Drain the pasta and add it to the sauce. Mix well and cook for 2 minutes more.

4. Remove from the heat, divide the pasta onto individual plates, and top each serving with 1 or 2 tablespoons of ricotta. Garnish with the basil and serve hot.

ANOTHER PASTABILITY

Zucchini Pasta alla Norma: Although the traditional recipe is prepared with eggplant, summer brings an abundance of zucchini, so feel free to use that instead. Zucchini cooks faster, so reduce the simmer time in step 1 to 8 to 10 minutes.

LEMONY ANGEL HAIR

Serves 4

Prep time: 5 minutes **/ Cook time:** 15 minutes

5-Ingredient / 30 Minutes or Less / Pantry Pasta

A favored dish in Sicily, one of Italy's top growers of lemons, this pasta dish is light, refreshing, and particularly summery. It's also widely prepared and served in Campania and the Amalfi Coast, where the lemons are huge. Some recipes just use oil and butter, but unsurprisingly, it's more delicious with the cream.

Table salt

1 pound angel hair pasta

½ cup heavy (whipping) cream

2 tablespoons butter

1 tablespoon olive oil

Juice of 1 lemon

Grated zest of 2 lemons

½ cup freshly grated Parmesan cheese

Freshly ground black pepper (optional)

1. In a 6-quart pot over high heat, bring 4 quarts of salted water to a boil. Add the pasta, stir, and cook for about 2 minutes less than the box instructs to just under al dente.

2. Meanwhile, as the pasta cooks, in a large sauté pan or skillet over medium heat, combine the heavy cream, butter, olive oil, and lemon juice. Bring to a simmer and cook for 3 to 4 minutes.

3. Using a pasta fork, strain the pasta from the water and add it to the sauce. Add 2 to 3 tablespoons of pasta water to the sauce and cook for 2 minutes more.

4. Remove from the heat and stir in the lemon zest and Parmesan cheese. Top with pepper to taste (if using) and serve hot.

ANOTHER PASTABILITY

Lemony Angel Hair with Shrimp: Add some cleaned and deveined shrimp to the simmering mixture in step 2, and cook for 3 to 4 minutes, or until the shrimp turn pink.

ST. JOSEPH'S DAY PASTA

Serves 4 to 6

Prep time: 5 minutes **/ Cook time:** 15 minutes

5-Ingredient / 30 Minutes or Less / Pantry Pasta

Eaten year-round, but especially on March 19, the day Italy celebrates the feast day of St. Joseph, this humble dish calls for just a few ingredients. The name comes from the main ingredient used, the bread crumbs, which are said to resemble the sawdust left behind after a carpenter's workday. This pasta is also often served as a first course on Christmas Eve, a day Italians traditionally enjoy seafood recipes or other meatless dishes.

½ cup olive oil, divided, plus more as needed

2 cups unseasoned bread crumbs

Table salt

1 pound bucatini, spaghetti, fettuccini, or other long pasta

8 oil-packed anchovy fillets, chopped, oil they're packed in reserved

Red pepper flakes, for seasoning

1. In a large sauté pan or skillet over medium heat, heat ¼ cup of olive oil. Add the bread crumbs and stir with a wooden spoon. Toast the bread crumbs for 2 to 3 minutes until lightly browned. Set aside in a small bowl.

2. Meanwhile, in a 6-quart pot over high heat, bring 4 quarts of salted water to a boil. Add the pasta, stir, and cook for about 2 minutes less than the box instructs to just under al dente.

3. As the pasta cooks, in the same pan used for the bread crumbs, combine the remaining ¼ cup of olive oil, the anchovies and their oil, and red pepper flakes to taste. Cook over low heat until the oil is hot but not burning and the anchovies break down.

4. Reserve 2 to 3 tablespoons of pasta water, drain the pasta, and add the pasta to the sauté pan. Toss to coat evenly, adding the pasta water, or more olive oil, if the pasta looks dry. Cook for about 2 minutes more until the pasta is fully cooked to al dente.

5. Turn off the heat. Add most of the bread crumbs to the pasta, stirring to coat evenly. Season with more salt, if needed. Plate the pasta and top each dish with the remaining bread crumbs.

> **Cooking tip:** I find toasted bread crumbs much more flavorful than plain bread crumbs, so when you make this recipe, toast a double batch and refrigerate the rest. They're great for coating chicken for chicken Parmesan cutlets.

ANOTHER PASTABILITY

St. Joseph's Day Pasta with Raisins and Pine Nuts: Make this dish more satiating with some raisins and pine nuts. Add them to taste during step 1 while toasting the bread crumbs. These are typical Sicilian additions to this dish.

PASTA ALLA GRICIA

Serves 4

Prep time: 5 minutes / **Cook time:** 20 minutes

5-Ingredient / 30 Minutes or Less

Traditionally made with guanciale, or cured pig's cheek, *pasta alla gricia* is another traditional Roman dish adored throughout Italy. Pancetta, which comes from the pig's belly, is an acceptable alternative to guanciale, as it's readily available in the United States. If you can't find pre-diced pancetta, ask for a nice thick piece of pancetta at the deli counter that you can cube at home.

Table salt

1 pound penne, rigatoni, or other tubular pasta

1 tablespoon olive oil

8 ounces cubed pancetta

½ cup grated Pecorino Romano cheese

Freshly ground black pepper

1. In a 6-quart pot over high heat, bring 4 quarts of salted water to a boil. Add the pasta, stir, and cook for about 2 minutes less than the box instructs to just under al dente.

2. Meanwhile, in a large sauté pan or skillet over medium heat, heat the olive oil. Add the pancetta and cook for 7 to 10 minutes, stirring frequently, until crispy.

3. Remove 1 cup of pasta water and slowly and carefully add it to the pancetta. Cook the sauce for 3 to 4 minutes, or until the liquid has reduced slightly.

4. Reserve 2 tablespoons of pasta water, drain the pasta, and add the pasta to the pan, mixing well to coat the pasta in the sauce.

5. Remove the pan from the heat and add the Pecorino Romano cheese and pepper to taste, mixing well. If desired, add 1 or 2 more tablespoons of pasta water. Serve hot.

SPAGHETTI ALLA CARBONARA

Serves 4

Prep time: 5 minutes / **Cook time:** 15 minutes

5-Ingredient / 30 Minutes or Less

Pasta alla carbonara is an iconic Roman dish now enjoyed throughout Italy. It is believed this quick dish was a favorite of the *carbonari*, the charcoal workers, who would go home during their lunch break and enjoy this dish. For a creamier, denser carbonara, use four large yolks in place of the three whole eggs.

Table salt

1 pound spaghetti

3 large eggs

¼ cup grated Pecorino Romano cheese, plus more for serving

Freshly ground black pepper

6 ounces diced pancetta

3 tablespoons olive oil

1. In a 6-quart pot over high heat, bring 4 quarts of salted water to a boil. Add the pasta, stir, and cook for about 2 minutes less than the box instructs to just under al dente.

2. In a small bowl, whisk the eggs, Pecorino Romano cheese, and pepper to taste until mixed well. Set aside.

3. In a large skillet over medium heat, cook the pancetta for 6 to 7 minutes until crispy and the fat is rendered. Add the olive oil and heat for 4 to 5 minutes.

4. Drain the spaghetti and add it to the sauce, tossing well to coat the pasta.

5. Reduce the heat to very low and add the egg and cheese mixture, stirring constantly to avoid scrambling the eggs. Cook for 1 minute, stirring. Plate and top with additional Pecorino Romano cheese. Serve immediately while hot.

ANOTHER PASTABILITY

Spaghetti alla Carbonara Frittata: Whisk in a few extra eggs into any leftovers and cook them in an ovenproof skillet over medium heat until the eggs start to set and settle. Add some grated cheese and bake in a 375°F oven until everything is firm. Serve warm.

BUCATINI ALL'AMATRICIANA

Serves 4 to 6

Prep time: 10 minutes **/ Cook time:** 35 minutes

Conceived in Lazio, the home region to Rome, this recipe is not only a favorite of Romans but also the rest of Italy. The original recipe doesn't vary much, and it's considered sacrilege by many even to consider any modifications. That said, I've swapped the traditional guanciale, which is cured pork cheek, for the easier-to-find pancetta.

½ cup cubed pancetta

½ cup dry white wine

1 tablespoon olive oil

½ small onion, finely chopped

1 (28-ounce) can high-quality crushed tomatoes

Table salt

1 pound bucatini or spaghetti

½ cup grated Pecorino Romano cheese

1. In a large sauté pan or skillet over medium heat, cook the pancetta for 4 to 5 minutes, until some fat is rendered. With a slotted spoon, remove the pancetta from the pan and set aside on some clean paper towels, leaving the remaining fat in the pan.

2. Add the wine to the pan and let the alcohol reduce for 2 to 3 minutes.

3. Add the olive oil and onion and cook for 3 to 4 minutes, or until the onion becomes translucent. Carefully add the canned tomatoes (they will splatter) and pancetta. Cook, uncovered, for 15 to 18 minutes, stirring occasionally.

4. Meanwhile, in a 6-quart pot over high heat, bring 4 quarts of salted water to a boil. Add the pasta, stir, and cook for about 2 minutes less than the box instructs to just under al dente.

5. Reserve 2 to 3 tablespoons of pasta water and drain the pasta. Add the pasta and reserved pasta water to the sauce and cook for 2 minutes. Mix well so the pasta is fully coated.

6. Remove from the heat, stir in the Pecorino Romano cheese, and serve immediately while hot.

Pair it: A few Ricotta with Honey Crostini (page 137) would make a perfect appetizer to enjoy while your sauce cooks.

ANOTHER PASTABILITY

Bucatini All'Amatriciana with Fresh Tomatoes: If it's summertime, use fresh tomatoes while they are at their peak. Use 2 to 3 pounds of diced fresh tomatoes in place of the canned ones and cook for about 30 minutes total.

CHAPTER THREE

VEGETARIAN PASTAS

As the daughter of a greengrocer, I grew up eating an abundance of pastas with vegetables and legumes. The possibilities are endless! Broccoli, eggplant, tomato, and zucchini are just the beginning. Cannellini beans, chickpeas, and lentils also make delicious pasta accompaniments. The cheesy pastas and pastas with white sauces are a great occasional alternative to the healthier counterparts.

PASTA E FAGIOLI

Serves 4

Prep time: 5 minutes / **Cook time:** 20 minutes

5-Ingredient / 30 Minutes or Less

Pasta e fagioli, or pasta with beans, is a favorite Italian dish eaten from north to south. The possible variations to this economical recipe are countless. Some folks enjoy it soupy, whereas others enjoy a drier version. This recipe is less soupy; if you want a bit more broth, add more pasta water during step 3. If you don't have homemade tomato sauce on hand, use your favorite jarred sauce.

Table salt

8 ounces elbow macaroni or small shells

3 cups homemade tomato sauce, divided (see Pasta al Pomodoro, page 25)

2 (15.5-ounce) cans cannellini beans, drained and rinsed

Freshly grated Parmesan or Romano cheese, for serving (optional)

1. In a 5-quart pot over high heat, bring 3 quarts of salted water to a boil. Add the pasta, stir, and cook for about 2 minutes less than the box instructs to just under al dente.

2. Meanwhile, pour about 2¼ cups of tomato sauce into a large sauté pan or skillet over low heat. Add ½ cup of pasta water and the beans. Cook for 5 to 6 minutes, stirring constantly and gently. Taste and season with salt.

3. Drain the pasta and add it to the sauce. Mix well and cook for 2 minutes. Gently stir to keep the delicate beans intact. Remove from the heat and plate, topping each serving with about 1 tablespoon of the remaining ¾ cup of tomato sauce. Serve topped with the grated cheese (if using).

ANOTHER PASTABILITY

Pasta e Ceci: Chickpeas are a wonderful alternative to cannellini beans in this recipe. Follow the recipe as directed. Chickpeas are a bit sturdier than cannellini beans, so cook them for 2 to 3 minutes longer in the sauce than the cannellini beans.

DITALINI AND CHICKPEA SOUP

Serves 6

Prep time: 10 minutes / **Cook time:** 30 minutes

Winters are long and can be downright dreadful. My comfort foods during these months are definitely soups and stews. This Italian chickpea soup is one of my favorites. It's hearty, sturdy, and filling, and when paired with a nice slice of toasted bread, what more could you need? You can also use other beans instead of chickpeas. Chickpeas take just a few minutes longer to cook.

3 tablespoons olive oil, plus more for drizzling

½ small onion, diced

2 garlic cloves, minced

3 carrots, peeled and cut into ¼-inch dice

2 rosemary sprigs

2 tablespoons chopped fresh parsley

½ cup canned tomato sauce or canned crushed tomatoes

1 teaspoon salt

6 to 7 cups water

1 vegetarian bouillon cube

2 (15.5-ounce) cans chickpeas, drained and rinsed

8 ounces ditalini

Freshly grated Parmesan cheese, for serving (optional)

1. In a 6-quart pot over medium heat, heat the olive oil. Add the onion, garlic, carrots, rosemary, parsley, tomato sauce, and salt. Cook for 3 to 4 minutes, stirring, until everything becomes fragrant and the onion is translucent.

2. Add the water. Partially cover the pot and leave some room for the steam to escape. Bring to a full boil. Add the bouillon cube and chickpeas and cook for 15 minutes, semi-covered.

3. Add the ditalini and cook according to the box instructions until al dente. Remove the rosemary sprigs and discard. Plate the soup and top with the Parmesan cheese (if using) and drizzle with olive oil. Serve immediately while hot.

Prep tip: During winter months I make a lot of soups, and because most call for diced carrot and onion, I chop a bunch of each at a time, place them in an airtight container, and refrigerate for up to 1 week.

MINESTRONE WITH MINIATURE FARFALLE

Serves 4 to 6

Prep time: 10 minutes / **Cook time:** 30 minutes

The word *minestra* loosely translates to soup. There is no exact recipe for this vegetable soup, so you're free to use any vegetable or legume you like. If you prefer, you can omit the bouillon and water in this recipe and substitute stock. Cooking the pasta directly in the soup adds a thickness that would otherwise be missing if you cook the pasta separately.

2 tablespoons olive oil, plus more for drizzling

2 to 3 carrots, peeled and finely diced

2 celery stalks, finely diced

1 small onion, diced

2 tablespoons chopped fresh parsley

1 (14-ounce) can diced tomatoes

1½ teaspoons salt

6 to 7 cups cold water

1 vegetarian bouillon cube

2 potatoes, peeled and cut into ¼-inch dice

1 (12-ounce) bag frozen Italian green beans

8 ounces miniature farfalle or other small-cut pasta, such as shells or ditalini

1 (12-ounce) bag fresh spinach

Freshly grated Parmesan or Romano cheese, for serving (optional)

1. In a 6-quart pot over medium heat, heat the oil. Add the carrots, celery, onion, parsley, tomatoes with their juice, and salt. Cook for 3 to 4 minutes, stirring, until everything becomes fragrant and the onion is translucent.

2. Add the cold water. Partially cover the pot, leaving some room for the steam to escape. Bring to a full boil. Add the bouillon cube, potatoes, and green beans. Cook for 10 minutes, semi-covered.

3. Add the pasta and cook for 5 to 6 minutes. Add the spinach and cook for 2 to 3 minutes more until the pasta is al dente. Plate and top with the grated cheese (if using) and drizzle with olive oil. Serve immediately while hot.

Pair it: Garlic Bruschetta (page 138) would be perfect for dunking in this soup!

PASTA CAPRESE

Serves 4 to 6

Prep time: 10 minutes / **Cook time:** 15 minutes

5-Ingredient / 30 Minutes or Less

Freshness and simplicity at its best—that's the most accurate way to describe this summery pasta salad from the island of Capri, off the Amalfi Coast. The main ingredients include mozzarella, tomatoes, and basil. Add some pasta, and you have a full meal!

Table salt

1 pound fusilli, rotini, or other fun pasta shape

1 cup fresh basil leaves

¼ cup extra-virgin olive oil

2 pints cherry tomatoes, halved

1 teaspoon dried oregano

1 pound bocconcini (small) mozzarella balls, or 2 large mozzarella balls, chopped into large pieces

1. In a 6-quart pot over high heat, bring 4 quarts of salted water to a boil. Add the pasta, stir, and cook according to the instructions on the box to al dente. Drain.

2. In a food processor or blender, combine the basil and olive oil. Pulse for several minutes until the dressing is well blended.

3. In a medium bowl, gently stir together the tomatoes and 1 teaspoon of salt. Let marinate for 3 to 5 minutes. Add the oregano, mozzarella, cooked pasta, and dressing. Mix well to coat the ingredients. Serve at room temperature or cold.

Prep tip: The longer the salted tomatoes sit, the juicier they will become. Feel free to chop and marinate the tomatoes up to 1 hour ahead of time.

ANOTHER PASTABILITY

Spinach Pasta Caprese: Add 1 (12-ounce) bag fresh baby spinach to this salad for added vitamins and color.

PASTA WITH PUREED BELL PEPPERS

Serves 4 to 6

Prep time: 15 minutes **/ Cook time:** 25 minutes

I was leading a culinary tour of Puglia one September, and the delicious week included several cooking classes and winery visits. This was one recipe we prepared during class. We all enthusiastically enjoyed this colorful, unique, and flavorful dish.

¼ cup olive oil

6 large red bell peppers, cut into ½-inch cubes

3 vine-ripened tomatoes, quartered

2 garlic cloves, peeled

1 teaspoon salt, plus more for the pasta water

4 fresh basil leaves, plus more for garnish

1 teaspoon dried oregano

1 pound penne or other tubular pasta

1. In a large sauté pan or skillet over medium heat, heat the olive oil. Add the red bell peppers, tomatoes, garlic, salt, basil, and oregano. Mix well. Cook for 15 to 20 minutes, or until the peppers are soft, reducing the heat if the oil dries up too quickly.

2. Meanwhile, in a 6-quart pot over high heat, bring 4 quarts of salted water to a boil. Add the pasta, stir, and cook for about 2 minutes less than the box instructs to just under al dente.

3. Transfer the cooked bell pepper and tomato mixture to a blender or food processor and pulse until well blended and creamy in consistency. Transfer the sauce back to the sauté pan, add ¼ cup of pasta water, and bring to a low simmer.

4. Drain the pasta and add it to the sauce. Mix well to coat the pasta evenly and cook for 1 to 2 minutes more. Top with fresh basil to serve.

ANOTHER PASTABILITY

Pasta with Roasted Pepper Puree: Roasting the same vegetables in the broiler delivers an entirely different flavor. Arrange all the ingredients (except the pasta) on a baking sheet and broil for 10 minutes, until the peppers are blistered and soft. Continue with step 2 onward.

MINIATURE SHELLS WITH PEAS AND ONIONS

Serves 4

Prep time: 10 minutes / **Cook time:** 20 minutes

5-Ingredient / 30 Minutes or Less

Ask any Italian what they eat on Fridays during Lent, and many will respond with "pasta and peas." This staple is a regular in many Italian households. In fact, frozen peas are the most frequently purchased frozen vegetable in Italy.

3 tablespoons olive oil

½ small onion, diced

1 pound frozen peas

1 teaspoon salt, plus more for the pasta water

1 cup water

8 ounces miniature shells

Freshly grated Parmesan or Pecorino Romano cheese (optional)

1. In a large sauté pan or skillet over medium heat, heat the olive oil. Add the onion and sauté for about 5 minutes until soft. Add the peas, salt, and water, reduce the heat to low, and cook for 8 to 10 minutes, depending on your preferred doneness.

2. Meanwhile, in a 5-quart pot over high heat, bring 3 quarts of salted water to a boil. Add the pasta, stir, and cook for about 2 minutes less than the box instructs to just under al dente.

3. Drain the shells and add them to the peas, mix well, and cook for 2 to 3 minutes. Plate and top with the grated cheese (if using).

> **Prep tip:** Does chopping onions make you cry? Freeze the onion for 30 minutes before chopping. Cold onions release their chemical gas more slowly, making the process a bit easier on the eyes.

ANOTHER PASTABILITY

Miniature Shells with Lima Beans and Onions: Not feeling the peas? Try frozen lima beans.

TAGLIATELLE WITH PORCINI MUSHROOMS

Serves 4

Prep time: 15 minutes / **Cook time:** 15 minutes

30 Minutes or Less

What better way to celebrate fall than with mushroom-based dishes? This is a classic dish that hits the tables in many Italian homes starting in September. It's a hearty, savory dish easily prepared within minutes.

2 tablespoons olive oil

1 tablespoon butter

1 pound porcini mushrooms, sliced

1 garlic clove, minced

¼ cup dry white wine

¼ teaspoon salt, plus more for the pasta water

Freshly ground black pepper

1 pound tagliatelle

1 tablespoon chopped fresh parsley

Freshly grated Parmesan cheese, for serving (optional)

1. In a large sauté pan or skillet over medium heat, heat the olive oil and melt the butter.

2. Add the mushrooms, garlic, white wine, salt, and pepper to taste. Cook, uncovered, for about 10 minutes, stirring occasionally.

3. Meanwhile, in a 6-quart pot over high heat, bring 4 quarts of salted water to a boil. Add the pasta, stir, and cook for about 2 minutes less than the box instructs to just under al dente.

4. Reserve ¼ cup of pasta water, drain the pasta, and add the pasta to the pan.

5. Add the parsley and cook for 2 to 3 minutes more until the pasta is fully cooked. If the pasta looks dry, add a few tablespoons of pasta water. Top with the Parmesan cheese (if using). Serve immediately while hot.

ANOTHER PASTABILITY

Tagliatelle with Portabella Mushrooms in Cream Sauce: Swap the porcinis for portabella mushrooms. Add 1 cup heavy (whipping) cream at the start of step 2 for a creamy sauce.

CLASSIC PASTA PRIMAVERA

Serves 6 to 8

Prep time: 15 minutes / **Cook time:** 20 minutes

Pasta primavera means springtime pasta in Italian, and like most pasta salads, there is no exact or original recipe for this dish. This delicious dish is ideal for picnics or as a great first course during summer barbecues. Short pasta shapes work best with chopped vegetables. Feel free to improvise—subtract or add as many vegetables as you want.

Table salt

1 pound farfalle, rotini, fusilli, or other short pasta of choice

¼ cup olive oil, plus more as needed

2 zucchini, diced

1 red bell pepper, diced

1 yellow bell pepper, diced

1 pound asparagus, trimmed and quartered

1 small onion, diced

2 small vine-ripened tomatoes, diced

5 or 6 fresh basil leaves

1 teaspoon dried oregano

1. In a 6-quart pot over high heat, bring 4 quarts of salted water to a boil. Add the pasta, stir, and cook according to the instructions on the box to al dente.

2. In a large sauté pan or skillet over medium heat, heat the olive oil. Add the zucchini, red and yellow bell peppers, asparagus, onion, tomatoes, basil, and oregano. Season with salt to taste. Cook for about 15 minutes until the vegetables are cooked to your desired doneness (tasting along the way). Stir occasionally to ensure the vegetables are not drying out or sticking to the pan, adding a tablespoon of olive oil or a few tablespoons of pasta water, if necessary.

3. Turn off the heat under the vegetables. Drain the pasta and add it to the sauté pan. Mix well. Transfer to a large serving bowl and serve family style.

ANOTHER PASTABILITY

Creamy Pasta Primavera: Add a delicious creamy dressing! In a small bowl, whisk ¼ cup heavy (whipping) cream, ¼ cup finely grated Parmesan cheese, and the grated zest of 1 lemon until smooth. Pour over the pasta right before serving.

ELBOWS WITH CHICKPEAS AND SPINACH IN RED SAUCE

Serves 6

Prep time: 15 minutes / **Cook time:** 25 minutes

5-Ingredient

Whole, ground, or pureed, Italians have enjoyed chickpeas, also known as garbanzo beans, or *ceci* in Italian, for centuries. An economical protein substitute for more expensive meats, this ingredient was a staple during harsher times.

Table salt

8 ounces elbow macaroni or miniature shells

2 cups homemade tomato sauce (see Pasta al Pomodoro, page 25)

2 (15.5-ounce) cans chickpeas, drained and rinsed

2 (12-ounce) bags fresh spinach, washed

Freshly grated Parmesan cheese, for serving (optional)

Olive oil

1. In a 5-quart pot over high heat, bring 3 quarts of salted water to a boil. Add the pasta, stir, and cook for about 2 minutes less than the box instructs to just under al dente.

2. In a large sauté pan or skillet over medium heat, combine the tomato sauce, chickpeas, and 1 cup of pasta water. Cook for 13 to 18 minutes, or until the chickpeas reach your desired consistency.

3. Add the spinach and cook for 3 or 4 minutes to wilt.

4. Reserve ¼ cup of pasta water, drain the pasta, and add the pasta to the sauté pan. Mix everything well, and stir in 2 to 3 tablespoons of the reserved pasta water. Top with the Parmesan cheese (if using) and a drizzle of olive oil. Serve immediately while hot.

ANOTHER PASTABILITY

Elbows with Cannellini Beans and Chard: One variation uses cannellini beans and Swiss chard instead of chickpeas and spinach. Because chard is tougher than spinach, parboil the chopped chard before adding it in step 3.

GRANDMA'S CAVATELLI WITH POTATOES

Serves 4

Prep time: 10 minutes / **Cook time:** 30 minutes

Pasta and potatoes is a cherished winter combination served by many in Italy. It's considered a peasant meal due to the low cost of the everyday ingredients used. It seems that every nonna has her own version, and as with many Italian recipes, adaptation is not only welcomed, but also encouraged.

3 tablespoons olive oil, plus more for drizzling

1 small onion, diced

2 garlic cloves, minced

1 carrot, peeled and diced

¼ cup canned crushed tomatoes

1 teaspoon salt

1 teaspoon dried oregano

4 potatoes, peeled and cut into ½-inch cubes

½ cup dry white wine

8 ounces cavatelli

Freshly grated Parmesan cheese, for serving (optional)

1. In a 6-quart pot over medium heat, heat the olive oil. Add the onion, garlic, carrot, tomatoes, and salt. Cook for 3 to 4 minutes, stirring, until everything becomes fragrant and the onion is translucent. Stir in the oregano.

2. Add the potatoes and white wine. Let the wine reduce for 2 to 3 minutes. Add enough water to cover the potatoes by about 3 inches. Cover the pot and cook for about 13 minutes until the potatoes are firm but not fully cooked.

3. Add the cavatelli and cook according to the instructions on the package. If the potatoes have dried too much to add the cavatelli, add hot water as needed.

4. Plate and top with the Parmesan cheese (if using). Serve immediately while hot.

ANOTHER PASTABILITY

Cavatelli with Sweet Potatoes: Sweet potatoes offer an interesting and colorful alternative in this recipe. Try it both ways to see which you prefer.

CAVATELLI WITH BROCCOLI PESTO

Serves 4 to 6

Prep time: 15 minutes **/ Cook time:** 15 minutes

30 Minutes or Less

Broccoli has always been one of my favorite vegetables, but it's not a very versatile ingredient, and sometimes it needs a little help to build its flavor profile. Preparing broccoli as a pesto is an inventive way to use this rustic vegetable. Feel free to swap the almonds for another nut, such as pecans, walnuts, or additional pine nuts.

1½ pounds broccoli florets

½ teaspoon salt, plus more for the pasta water

1 pound cavatelli or other pasta of choice

10 large fresh basil leaves

¼ cup pine nuts

¼ cup almonds

¼ cup freshly grated Parmesan or Romano cheese, plus more for serving

¼ cup extra-virgin olive oil, plus more as needed

1. Fill a bowl with ice and water and set aside. Place a medium pot full of water over high heat and bring to a boil. Add the broccoli florets and blanch for 3 to 4 minutes. Remove them from the water and add them to the ice bath to stop the cooking and maintain their color. Remove from the ice bath and dry with a paper towel. Place the florets in a food processor.

2. Meanwhile, in a 6-quart pot over high heat, bring 4 quarts of salted water to a boil. Add the pasta, stir, and cook according to the instructions on the box to al dente.

3. To the food processor, add the basil, pine nuts, almonds, Parmesan cheese, and salt. Pulse a few times. While pulsing, slowly stream in the olive oil, continuing to pulse until creamy. If the pesto looks dry, add another tablespoon or so of oil. Transfer the pesto to a large serving bowl.

4. Drain the pasta, reserving a little pasta water, and add the pasta to the pesto. Mix well to coat evenly. Add 1 tablespoon of pasta water or olive oil if the pasta looks dry. Top with the grated cheese. Serve at room temperature.

ANOTHER PASTABILITY

Orecchiette with Broccoli Pesto and Ricotta: Mix ¼ cup whole-milk ricotta into the pesto and swap the cavatelli for orecchiette for a completely different dish.

GNOCCHI WITH MOZZARELLA

Serves 4

Prep time: 15 minutes / **Cook time:** 20 minutes

Eating this dish always takes me back to the Campania region of Italy; more specifically, to my culinary tours on the Amalfi Coast. Both mozzarella and gnocchi are staples in this part of Italy and eaten very often, so enjoying this dish brings back those nice memories.

3 tablespoons olive oil

2 pints cherry tomatoes, halved

2 scallions, or ½ small onion, diced

½ teaspoon salt, plus more for the gnocchi water

1 pound shelf-stable gnocchi

1 (8-ounce) mozzarella ball, squeezed dry and cut into ¼-inch dice

3 fresh basil leaves, chopped

Freshly ground black pepper

2 tablespoons freshly grated Parmesan cheese

1. In a large sauté pan or skillet over medium heat, heat the olive oil. Add the tomatoes, scallions, and salt. Reduce the heat to medium-low and sauté for about 15 minutes, or until the tomatoes have popped and create a saucy consistency.

2. Meanwhile, in a 6-quart pot over high heat, bring 4 quarts of salted water to a boil. Add the gnocchi, stir, and cook according to the instructions on the box. Drain.

3. Place the mozzarella cubes into a serving bowl. Add the cooked gnocchi, cooked tomatoes, and basil. Season with salt and pepper to taste and mix to incorporate all the ingredients. Top with Parmesan cheese and serve hot or at room temperature.

ANOTHER PASTABILITY

Gnocchi with Artichoke Hearts: For a more substantial dish, add frozen artichoke hearts to the tomatoes while they cook. Add them right after the scallions and cook for the duration that the sauce cooks.

GEMELLI WITH FRESH TOMATO SAUCE

Serves 4 to 6

Prep time: 30 minutes **/ Cook time:** 35 minutes

5-Ingredient

Growing up in southern Italy, I was fortunate to have access to delicious organic produce year-round. Since my dad was a greengrocer, we certainly never lacked for fresh vegetables and fruits. The bounty really came to life in summer when tomatoes were at their peak. One summer dish that was always on rotation in my mom's kitchen was a fresh tomato sauce. This sauce was the base for many dishes throughout the week, but simply tossed with some gemelli was the most delicious way to enjoy it.

4 to 5 pounds vine-ripened tomatoes

3 tablespoons olive oil

3 garlic cloves, minced

6 large fresh basil leaves, chopped, plus more for garnish

½ teaspoon salt, plus more for the pasta water

1 pound gemelli or other pasta of choice

Freshly grated Parmesan cheese, for serving (optional)

1. Fill a large bowl with water and ice and set aside. In a 6-quart pot over high heat, bring 4 quarts of water to a boil. With a small paring knife, carefully cut an **X** at the bottom of each tomato. Using a slotted spoon or spider, carefully lower each tomato into the boiling water and boil for about 30 seconds. Carefully remove each tomato from the boiling water and place in the ice water. Continue until all the tomatoes are blanched.

2. Remove the outer skin from the tomatoes; it should start peeling easily where the **X** was made. Quarter the peeled tomatoes and remove as many of the seeds as possible (it's okay if a few seeds make it into the sauce), and place the chopped tomatoes in a bowl.

3. In a large sauté pan or skillet over medium heat, heat the olive oil. Add the garlic, basil, and salt. Sauté for 2 to 3 minutes. Add the tomatoes and cook for about 25 minutes, uncovered, stirring occasionally. The tomatoes will break down while cooking.

4. Meanwhile, in the 6-quart pot over high heat, bring 4 quarts of salted water to a boil. Add the pasta, stir, and cook for about 2 minutes less than the box instructs to just under al dente.

5. Scoop out about a ½ cup of sauce and place it in a small bowl.

6. Drain the pasta and add it to the remaining sauce in the pan. Cook for about 3 minutes, stirring to coat the pasta then plate and top each serving with 2 tablespoons of the reserved sauce and a few more basil leaves. Top with the Parmesan cheese (if using). Serve immediately while hot.

Pair it: In keeping with the theme of fresh tomatoes, pair this dish with Stuffed Tomatoes (page 141). They make a wonderful antipasto to this dish.

PASTA ALLA SORRENTINA

Serves 4 to 6

Prep time: 10 minutes / **Cook time:** 30 minutes

Each region you visit in Italy has its own favored dishes. In Sorrento, in the region of Campania, gnocchi or pasta *alla sorrentina* is sure to be on any restaurant menu and prepared in many homes. The base for this dish is a simple tomato sauce and fresh mozzarella. The best part of this dish is the crunchy topping, but don't stray too far while this is in your broiler, as it can go from crunchy to burnt in no time!

2 tablespoons olive oil

2 garlic cloves, peeled

1 (28-ounce) can crushed tomatoes

1 teaspoon salt, plus more for the pasta water

5 or 6 fresh basil leaves, roughly chopped

Nonstick cooking spray

1 pound penne, rigatoni, or other tubular pasta

1 (8-ounce) fresh mozzarella ball, squeezed of excess liquid, and cut into ¼-inch dice

½ cup freshly grated Parmesan cheese

1. In a large sauté pan or skillet over medium heat, heat the olive oil and garlic for 2 minutes. Add the tomatoes, salt, and basil. Reduce the heat to low and simmer the sauce, uncovered, for 15 to 20 minutes, stirring occasionally. Remove the garlic and discard.

2. Place an oven rack on the highest level possible and preheat the broiler. If your oven does not have a broil setting, preheat it to the highest temperature. Coat a 9-by-10-inch baking dish with cooking spray and set aside.

3. Meanwhile, in a 6-quart pot over high heat, bring 4 quarts of salted water to a boil. Add the pasta, stir, and cook for about 2 minutes less than the box instructs to just under al dente.

4. Drain the pasta and add it to the sauce. Mix well to coat the pasta evenly with the sauce. Layer half the pasta in the prepared baking dish. Top the pasta with half the mozzarella. Cover the mozzarella with the remaining pasta and top the pasta with the remaining mozzarella. Sprinkle the Parmesan cheese on top.

5. Broil the pasta for 5 to 7 minutes until the cheese forms a crunchy, melted topping. Serve immediately.

Prep tip: It's important to squeeze out as much liquid as possible from the mozzarella. Wrap the mozzarella in paper towels and squeeze it to remove excess liquid.

ANOTHER PASTABILITY

Gnocchi alla Sorrentina: Make this using 1 pound store-bought, shelf-stable gnocchi instead of the pasta.

SPAGHETTI WITH MUSHROOM CARBONARA

Serves 4 to 6

Prep time: 15 minutes / **Cook time:** 20 minutes

The original carbonara is an Italian classic adored by many, but as home chefs got creative, new variations were developed. Although the classic version (Spaghetti alla Carbonara, page 43) reigns supreme, this version is enjoyed by vegetarians and meat eaters alike.

Table salt

1 pound spaghetti or other long, thin pasta

4 large egg yolks

½ cup freshly grated Parmesan cheese

Freshly ground black pepper

¼ cup olive oil

1 pound cremini mushrooms, stemmed and quartered

2 garlic cloves, minced

1 teaspoon chopped fresh parsley

1. In a 6-quart pot over high heat, bring 4 quarts of salted water to a boil. Add the pasta, stir, and cook for about 2 minutes less than the box instructs to just under al dente.

2. In a small bowl, whisk the egg yolks, Parmesan cheese, and pepper to taste. Set aside.

3. Meanwhile, as the pasta cooks, in a large sauté pan or skillet over medium heat, heat the olive oil. Add the mushrooms, garlic, and parsley. Cook for 5 to 7 minutes, stirring often. Taste and season with salt.

4. Add ¾ cup of pasta water to the mushrooms. Reserve an additional ¼ cup of water, then drain the pasta. Add the pasta to the sauté pan, mixing well.

5. Add a few tablespoons of reserved pasta water to the egg and cheese mixture. Mix well and vigorously to avoid scrambling the eggs. Remove the sauté pan from the heat and quickly add the egg mixture to the sauté pan while continuing to mix the ingredients. The heat from the pasta water and the pan will safely cook the egg mixture. Add the parsley, plate, and serve immediately while hot.

Prep tip: Mushrooms are like sponges; they soak up a lot of water, so it's best to avoid washing them under running water. Instead, wipe them with a wet paper towel to remove any visible dirt.

ANOTHER PASTABILITY

Zucchini Carbonara: A wonderful alternative uses diced zucchini instead of mushrooms. Follow the recipe as directed, add some basil leaves, if available, and transform this fall dish into summer deliciousness.

BAKED ITALIAN MAC AND CHEESE

Serves 6 to 8

Prep time: 15 minutes **/ Cook time:** 30 minutes

Worth the Wait

Italians don't really have a version of "mac and cheese" as we know it in the United States. They do bake lots of pastas and use cheese as a base, but it's hardly what we know here. That said, this version is cheesy, melty, and quick enough to make any night of the week. This is sure to become a new family favorite. If you don't have Fontina cheese, swap it for 2 ounces more of provolone, mozzarella, or a combination.

Nonstick cooking spray

Table salt

1 pound penne, ziti, or rigatoni

4 tablespoons (½ stick) butter (salted or unsalted)

¼ cup all-purpose flour

2 cups whole-milk or heavy (whipping) cream

4 ounces sliced provolone cheese, diced

4 ounces shredded mozzarella cheese

2 ounces Fontina cheese

½ cup freshly grated Parmesan cheese

1. Preheat the oven to 375°F. Coat a 9-by-13-inch baking dish with cooking spray. Set aside.

2. In a 6-quart pot over high heat, bring 4 quarts of salted water to a boil. Add the pasta, stir, and cook for 4 minutes less than instructed on the box. Drain and transfer to a large bowl.

3. Meanwhile, in a large sauté pan or skillet over medium heat, melt the butter. Add the flour and mix well. Add the milk and cook for about 5 minutes, stirring, until the milk is hot, but not boiling. Look for small bubbles forming around the edges of the pan.

4. Add the provolone, mozzarella, and Fontina cheeses and mix well until everything is combined and the cheeses melt.

5. Add the drained pasta to the sauce, mixing well to coat. Pour the pasta and cheese into the prepared baking dish and spread it evenly. Top with the Parmesan cheese.

6. Bake for 20 minutes until a crunchy top forms. Serve immediately while hot.

ANOTHER PASTABILITY

Baked Italian Mac and Cheese with Broccoli: A wonderful supplement to this dish is the addition of some vegetables. Add a few cups of frozen broccoli florets to the boiling pasta during the last 4 minutes of cooking and continue with the recipe as directed.

ZUCCHINI PASTA BAKE WITH BÉCHAMEL SAUCE

Serves 6 to 8

Prep time: 20 minutes **/ Cook time:** 40 minutes

5-Ingredient / Worth the Wait

Many traditional baked pasta dishes call for red sauce, but you can deviate from that and use a white sauce instead. This summer recipe uses one of Italy's most adored vegetables, zucchini. Of course, this dish can also be made with a red sauce—try it both ways!

Nonstick cooking spray

Table salt

1 pound rotini, fusilli, or farfalle

¼ cup olive oil

3 zucchini, diced

2 cups peas

1 garlic clove, minced

Freshly ground black pepper

2¼ cups Béchamel Sauce (see Pasta with Béchamel Sauce, page 32)

1. Preheat the oven to 375°F. Coat a 9-by-13-inch baking dish with cooking spray. Set aside.

2. Meanwhile, in a 6-quart pot over high heat, bring 4 quarts of salted water to a boil. Add the pasta, stir, and cook for 4 minutes less than instructed on the box.

3. In a large sauté pan or skillet over medium heat, heat the olive oil. Add the zucchini, peas, and garlic and season with salt and pepper to taste. Sauté for 10 to 15 minutes until the vegetables are cooked through, depending on your preference for doneness.

4. Drain the pasta and add it to the vegetables. Turn off the heat and stir in the béchamel sauce, mixing until well incorporated. Spread the pasta into the prepared baking dish.

5. Bake for 20 to 25 minutes, or until the top is lightly browned and the corners are crisp. Serve immediately while hot.

EGGPLANT PASTA BAKE

Serves 6 to 8

Prep time: 15 minutes / **Cook time:** 35 minutes

Worth the Wait

Baking a pasta recipe elevates the dish to a completely different level. The crunchy topping and the crispy corners make it that much more appealing.

¼ cup olive oil

1 large eggplant, cubed

2 red bell peppers, cut into ¼-inch dice

2 ripe tomatoes, diced

1 small onion, diced

1 teaspoon salt, plus more for the pasta water

1 teaspoon dried oregano

Nonstick cooking spray

1 pound ziti or penne

2 large eggs, hardboiled, peeled, quartered, and diced

¼ cup freshly grated Parmesan cheese

¼ cup bread crumbs

1. In a large sauté pan or skillet over medium heat, heat the olive oil. Add the eggplant, red bell peppers, tomatoes, onion, salt, and oregano. Stir-fry for 10 to 12 minutes until the vegetables are soft and tender. If they are drying up too quickly, reduce the heat and add about ¼ cup water, a bit at a time, as needed.

2. Preheat the oven to 375°F. Coat a 9-by-13-inch baking dish with cooking spray.

3. In a 6-quart pot over high heat, bring 4 quarts of salted water to a boil. Add the pasta, stir, and cook for 4 minutes less than instructed on the box.

4. Drain the pasta and add to the sauté pan. Mix well and transfer to the prepared baking dish. Top with the hardboiled eggs, evenly spaced over the pasta, and sprinkle with the Parmesan cheese and bread crumbs.

5. Bake for 20 minutes, or until the top is browned. Serve hot or at room temperature.

ANOTHER PASTABILITY

Zucchini Pasta Bake: Swap the eggplant for zucchini. Follow the recipe as directed but reduce the cook time in step 1 to 7 or 8 minutes.

CHAPTER FOUR

FISH AND SEAFOOD

Growing up in Calabria, surrounded by the Ionian and Tyrrhenian Seas, I remember how our meals often consisted of seafood. Freshly caught swordfish was one of my favorites and still is today. Other frequently enjoyed seafood included clams, cod, prawns, and scallops. One of the many benefits of seafood is how quickly it cooks. When it comes to pantry seafood, my go-tos are tuna packed in olive oil, sardines, and anchovies. If you're new to cooking pasta with seafood, this chapter will show you how easy it is. One thing you'll notice is the lack of grated cheeses. Although you certainly can add grated cheese to finish your pasta, it is not frequently combined with seafood in Italy.

ORZO SALAD WITH TUNA AND OLIVES

Serves 4

Prep time: 15 minutes **/ Cook time:** 15 minutes

30 Minutes or Less

Orzo is perhaps one of my favorite tiny pastas. A great addition to soups, orzo is also wonderful in place of rice in mock risottos and in salads. This tasty salad comes together quickly and is ideal as a light first course. It also makes great leftovers for lunch the next day!

Table salt

8 ounces orzo

2 tablespoons olive oil, plus more for drizzling

½ small onion, minced

2 (5-ounce) cans oil-packed tuna

1 pint cherry tomatoes, halved

½ cup Sicilian or Greek olives, pitted and quartered

½ cup dry white wine

1 tablespoon chopped fresh parsley

Freshly ground black pepper

1. In a 5-quart pot over high heat, bring 3 quarts of salted water to a boil. Add the pasta, stir, and cook for about 2 minutes less than the box instructs to just under al dente.

2. In a large sauté pan or skillet over medium heat, heat the olive oil. Add the onion and sauté for 2 to 3 minutes. Add the tuna and the oil it came in, tomatoes, and olives. Cook for 3 to 4 minutes.

3. Add the white wine and let reduce for 2 to 3 minutes. Season with the parsley and pepper to taste.

4. Drain the orzo and add it to the sauté pan. Toss everything for a few minutes and finish with an additional drizzle of olive oil.

ANOTHER PASTABILITY

Penne Salad with Tuna and Anchovies: For a creative alternative, cook as directed, but replace the orzo for something more satiating, like penne, and swap the olives for anchovies.

FETTUCCINI IN TUNA SAUCE

Serves 4 to 6

Prep time: 5 minutes / **Cook time:** 20 minutes

5-Ingredient / 30 Minutes or Less

You come home after a long day and realize you've got a minimal supply of groceries. You haven't taken anything out of the freezer; you haven't gone shopping in a week; and the thought of preparing anything too complex or time-consuming is daunting. Opening your cupboards and fridge, you realize you have everything you need for this delicious tuna sauce. You're in luck—this satisfying dish is only minutes away, and it's delicious.

Table salt

1 pound fettuccini

2 tablespoons olive oil

½ small onion, finely diced

2 (5-ounce) cans oil-packed tuna, drained, oil reserved

1 (28-ounce) can crushed tomatoes

5 or 6 fresh basil leaves, chopped

Freshly ground black pepper

1. In a 6-quart pot over high heat, bring 4 quarts of salted water to a boil. Add the pasta, stir, and cook for about 2 minutes less than the box instructs to just under al dente.

2. Meanwhile, as the pasta cooks, in a large sauté pan or skillet over medium heat, heat the olive oil. Add the onion, oil from the tuna, and salt to taste. Sauté for 2 to 3 minutes. Add the canned tuna and, using a wooden spoon, break it apart. Cook for 1 to 2 minutes.

3. Stir in the tomatoes and reduce the heat to medium-low. Cook, covered, for 15 minutes, stirring occasionally.

4. Reserve a few tablespoons of pasta water, drain the pasta, and add the pasta to the sauce. Stir in the pasta water and cook for 2 to 3 minutes more.

5. Add the basil leaves, season with pepper to taste, and serve immediately while hot.

Prep tip: Drain the tuna in a colander for several minutes to get out the most oil for maximum flavor.

SPAGHETTI WITH SARDINES

Serves 4 to 6

Prep time: 10 minutes / **Cook time:** 15 minutes

30 Minutes or Less

This recipe is a Sicilian staple. It's often eaten during Lent, when many abstain from eating meat on Fridays. This dish packs lots of flavor, but you can use canned mackerel instead for milder taste.

Table salt

1 pound spaghetti or other long pasta

4 tablespoons olive oil, divided

½ cup bread crumbs

1 small onion, finely chopped

Freshly ground black pepper

2 (4-ounce) cans olive oil–packed sardines

2 tablespoons capers, rinsed and drained

¼ cup black olives, pitted and roughly chopped

2 tablespoons chopped fresh parsley

1. In a 6-quart pot over high heat, bring 4 quarts of salted water to a boil. Add the pasta, stir, and cook for about 2 minutes less than the box instructs to just under al dente.

2. Meanwhile, as the pasta cooks, in a large sauté pan or skillet over medium heat, heat 2 tablespoons of olive oil. Add the bread crumbs and cook, stirring, until toasted. Remove from the heat and set aside.

3. In the same pan, heat the remaining 2 tablespoons of olive oil and add the onion. Season with salt and pepper to taste and cook for 3 to 4 minutes until the onion is translucent.

4. Add the sardines and the oil they are packed in, breaking them up with a wooden spoon. Stir in the capers and olives and cook for 3 to 4 minutes.

5. Reserve about ¼ cup of pasta water, drain the pasta, and add the pasta to the sauté pan. Cook for several minutes, mixing well to coat in the sauce. Stir in the pasta water. Remove from the heat, mix in the toasted bread crumbs and parsley, and serve immediately while hot.

VERMICELLI WITH SWISS CHARD AND ANCHOVIES

Serves 4 to 6

Prep time: 15 minutes / **Cook time:** 20 minutes

5-Ingredient

I love mixing vegetables with seafood dishes, but not many vegetables work well with seafood, so creating new recipes requires a little ingenuity. Swiss chard is one of my favorite vegetables and it's widely used in Italy, so pairing it with canned anchovies seemed fitting.

1 pound Swiss chard, stemmed and chopped into 1-inch pieces	1 pound vermicelli or other long, thin pasta	Freshly ground black pepper
Table salt	2 tablespoons olive oil	2 (2-ounce) cans olive oil–packed anchovies, chopped, oil reserved
	1 small onion, chopped	
	3 garlic cloves, minced	

1. Bring a medium pot of water to a boil over high heat. Add the Swiss chard and boil for 5 minutes. Drain and set aside.

2. In a 6-quart pot over high heat, bring 4 quarts of salted water to a boil. Add the pasta, stir, and cook for about 2 minutes less than the box instructs to just under al dente.

3. Meanwhile, as the pasta cooks, in a large sauté pan or skillet over medium heat, heat the olive oil. Add the onion and garlic. Season with salt and pepper to taste. Sauté for about 3 minutes.

4. Add the anchovies and the oil they came in to the garlic and onion and break down the anchovies with a wooden spoon. Stir in the Swiss chard, mixing well.

5. Reserve about ¼ cup of pasta water, drain the pasta, and add the pasta to the sauté pan. Stir well, then stir in the pasta water. Serve immediately while hot.

LINGUINI WITH CLAM SAUCE

Serves 4

Prep time: 10 minutes / **Cook time:** 15 minutes

30 Minutes or Less

Linguini with clam sauce is a classic Italian dish frequently served at home and on restaurant tables. It usually includes garlic, parsley, and white wine. You'll find that garlic and parsley are staples in many seafood dishes, as they complement each other well.

Table salt

1 pound linguini

2 pounds small clams, scrubbed clean

¼ cup olive oil

4 garlic cloves

Red pepper flakes, for seasoning

¾ cup dry white wine

1 tablespoon chopped fresh parsley

Freshly ground black pepper

1. In a 6-quart pot over high heat, bring 4 quarts of salted water to a boil. Add the pasta, stir, and cook for about 2 minutes less than the box instructs to just under al dente.

2. Sort the clams and attempt to close any that are open by giving them a quick tap. If they don't close, discard them.

3. In a large sauté pan or skillet over medium heat, heat the olive oil. Add the garlic and red pepper flakes to taste. Cook for 1 minute, stirring.

4. Add the clams and white wine, cover the pan, and cook for 5 minutes, or until the clams open. Discard any clams that remain closed.

5. Drain the linguini and add it to the sauce. Mix everything and add the parsley. Season with salt and pepper to taste. Serve immediately while hot.

ANOTHER PASTABILITY

Linguini in Red Clam Sauce: For a delicious red sauce to dress your linguini, add 1 (14.5-ounce) can crushed tomatoes to step 4, right after the wine, then cover and cook for 10 minutes.

PASTA WITH MUSSELS IN WHITE WINE

Serves 4 to 6

Prep time: 15 minutes / **Cook time:** 25 minutes

Mussels and wine, like clams and wine, are another classic combination made in culinary heaven. You'll note that the recipe calls for 3 pounds of mussels. This is not an exact amount, but as you know, much of the weight is in the shells, and you're likely going to have a few that don't open so you'll have to discard them. That said, 3 pounds serves 4 to 6 people at most.

2 cups dry white wine	Table salt	3 garlic cloves, minced
2 teaspoons dried oregano	1 pound spaghetti or other long pasta	2 tablespoons chopped fresh parsley
3 pounds mussels, cleaned and debearded	¼ cup olive oil	1 tablespoon butter

1. In a large stockpot over high heat, combine the wine, oregano, and mussels. Bring to a boil and cook for about 5 minutes, or until the mussels open. Drain the mussels, reserving the liquid. Discard any unopened mussels.

2. Remove the mussels from their shells and place them in a bowl. Set aside.

3. In a 6-quart pot over high heat, bring 4 quarts of salted water to a boil. Add the pasta, stir, and cook for about 2 minutes less than the box instructs to just under al dente.

4. In a large sauté pan or skillet over medium heat, heat the olive oil. Add the garlic and parsley and cook, stirring, for just 1 minute. Add the butter and slowly add the reserved mussels cooking liquid to the pan. Season with salt to taste and simmer the sauce for 5 to 7 minutes.

5. Drain the pasta and add it to the pan. Add the mussels to the sauce and toss several times until the pasta is well coated. Serve immediately while hot.

Cooking tip: The wine broth from step 1 may have some grit or sand at the bottom, so pour carefully and slowly, leaving behind the last bit of liquid containing anything unsavory.

ORZO PILAF WITH SHRIMP

Serves 4

Prep time: 15 minutes / **Cook time:** 35 minutes

I'm a big fan of risotto and have found that cooking orzo similarly to cooking risotto works very well and creates a lighter, more delicate result. This is a fun recipe for summer barbecues and get-togethers.

2½ cups vegetable broth

1 tablespoon tomato paste

¼ cup olive oil

1 large red bell pepper, cut into ¼-inch dice

1 small onion, diced

Table salt

Freshly ground black pepper

8 ounces orzo

1 cup dry white wine

8 ounces small shrimp, peeled and deveined

2 tablespoons chopped fresh parsley

1. In a medium saucepan over medium heat, heat the vegetable broth. Stir in the tomato paste to dissolve, remove from the heat, and set aside.

2. In a large sauté pan or skillet over medium heat, heat the olive oil. Add the red bell peppers and onion. Season with salt and pepper to taste. Cook for about 10 minutes until the vegetables have softened.

3. Add the orzo to the pan and toast the pasta for 3 to 4 minutes, mixing well and frequently so it does not burn. Add the white wine and let it reduce for 2 to 3 minutes.

4. Add the hot broth mixture, cover the pan, and cook for about 8 minutes, stirring occasionally (see cooking tip).

5. Add the shrimp and parsley. Cook for 3 to 4 minutes more until the shrimp turn pink and are fully cooked. Serve hot or at room temperature.

ANOTHER PASTABILITY

Orzo Pilaf with Zucchini and Shrimp: Zucchini and shrimp are a great combination. Swap the pepper for diced zucchini for a lighter dish and one that is quicker to prepare, as zucchini cooks in half the time.

RESTAURANT-STYLE SHRIMP SCAMPI WITH ANGEL HAIR

Serves 4

Prep time: 10 minutes / **Cook time:** 15 minutes

30 Minutes or Less

People are surprised to learn that shrimp scampi is not really an Italian dish but very much an Italian American invention. This dish is likely the creation of an Italian immigrant making use of new ingredients not easily found during olden times in Italy, such as butter.

Table salt

1 pound angel hair pasta

¼ cup olive oil, plus more as needed

1 pound large shrimp, peeled and deveined

2 garlic cloves, minced

Red pepper flakes, for seasoning

½ cup dry white wine

4 tablespoons (½ stick) butter

1 tablespoon chopped fresh parsley

1. In a 6-quart pot over high heat, bring 4 quarts of salted water to a boil. Add the pasta, stir, and cook for about 2 minutes less than the box instructs to just under al dente.

2. Meanwhile, as the pasta cooks, in a large sauté pan or skillet over medium heat, heat the olive oil. Add the shrimp and sauté for 2 to 3 minutes, or until pink. Add the garlic, red pepper flakes to taste, and white wine. Stir and let the wine reduce for 3 to 4 minutes. Season with salt to taste and add the butter, stirring until fully melted.

3. Reserve ½ cup of pasta water, drain the angel hair, and add the pasta to the sauce. Toss to coat evenly. Add 1 or 2 tablespoons of pasta water, or an additional drizzle of olive oil, if desired. Serve immediately while hot.

ANOTHER PASTABILITY

Shrimp Scampi with Lemon Sauce: Decrease the wine to ¼ cup, add ¼ cup freshly squeezed lemon juice, and finish with some grated lemon zest for a delicious, light, citrusy twist on this classic.

PASTA WITH ZUCCHINI PESTO AND PRAWNS

Serves 4

Prep time: 10 minutes, plus 15 minutes to rest / **Cook time:** 15 minutes

Zucchini with prawns (or shrimp) is an ideal dish in summer when both zucchini and basil are at their peak and we often turn to lighter meals. This delicate zucchini pesto over mostaccioli or ziti makes for a perfect weeknight dish!

2 zucchini

½ teaspoon salt, plus more for the pasta water

⅓ cup pine nuts

5 large fresh basil leaves

½ cup freshly grated Parmesan cheese

½ cup plus 2 tablespoons extra-virgin olive oil, divided

1 pound mostaccioli or ziti

1 garlic clove, minced

1 pound prawns, peeled and deveined

1. Using the coarse side of a box grater, shred the zucchini and place it in a colander lined with paper towels. Lightly salt the zucchini and set aside for 15 minutes to draw out some liquid.

2. Transfer the zucchini to a food processor. Add the pine nuts, basil, and Parmesan cheese and pulse several times. Stream in ½ cup of oil, pulsing, until creamy.

3. In a 6-quart pot over high heat, bring 4 quarts of salted water to a boil. Add the pasta, stir, and cook for about 2 minutes less than the box instructs to just under al dente.

4. Meanwhile, as the pasta cooks, in a large sauté pan or skillet over medium heat, heat the 2 remaining tablespoons of olive oil. Add the garlic and prawns and cook for 3 to 5 minutes, or until the prawns turn pink and are cooked.

5. Reserve 2 to 3 tablespoons of pasta water and drain the pasta. Reduce the heat to low and add the pasta and pasta water to the pan. Mix well. Cook for 2 to 3 minutes more.

6. Turn off the heat and stir in the pesto. Serve hot or at room temperature.

Prep tip: To make the prep easier, purchase peeled and deveined prawns. Your fishmonger is there to help and will be happy to assist you.

SHRIMP PARMESAN

Serves 4 to 6

Prep time: 15 minutes / **Cook time:** 25 minutes

Eggplant Parmigiana, better known as "eggplant parm" in the United States, is a classic Italian dish from the island of Sicily. But much like the chicken version, shrimp parm is an Italian American invention. It's delicious and requires far less work than the more laborious original version with eggplant.

3 cups homemade tomato sauce (see Pasta al Pomodoro, page 25)

¾ cup bread crumbs

¼ cup freshly grated Parmesan cheese

½ teaspoon salt, plus more for the pasta water

2 large eggs, lightly beaten

1½ to 2 pounds large shrimp, peeled and deveined

1 pound spaghetti, angel hair, linguini, or other long pasta

3 tablespoons olive oil

½ cup shredded mozzarella cheese

1. Preheat the oven to broil. If your oven doesn't have a broil setting, preheat to the highest temperature.

2. Pour 1 cup of tomato sauce into a 9-by-11-inch baking pan and set aside.

3. In a small bowl, using your fingers or a fork, mix the bread crumbs, Parmesan cheese, and salt.

4. Place the beaten eggs in a shallow bowl. Dip the shrimp in the beaten eggs, then in the bread crumb mixture to coat evenly.

5. In a 6-quart pot over high heat, bring 4 quarts of salted water to a boil. Add the pasta, stir, and cook for about 2 minutes less than the box instructs to just under al dente. Drain.

6. In a large sauté pan or skillet over medium heat, heat the olive oil. Working in batches, carefully add the shrimp to the hot oil and fry on one side for 2 to 3 minutes, turn, and fry on the other side for about 2 minutes until golden brown.

7. Transfer the cooked shrimp to the baking dish with the tomato sauce. Top the shrimp with the mozzarella cheese.

8. Broil for 2 to 3 minutes until the cheese melts.

9. Add the remaining 2 cups of tomato sauce to the sauté pan used for the shrimp. Heat the sauce and add the drained pasta, tossing to mix well. Transfer the pasta to a large serving bowl, top with the shrimp, and serve family style.

Prep tip: The shrimp can be battered up to a few hours in advance. Refrigerate until ready to cook. If you don't have homemade tomato sauce on hand, jarred marinara will work in a pinch.

FETTUCCINI WITH SCALLOPS AND WHITE WINE SAUCE

Serves 4

Prep time: 10 minutes / **Cook time:** 20 minutes

30 Minutes or Less

Seafood dishes come together quickly, easily, and often with just a few ingredients. The scallops in this gourmet recipe are crispy on the outside and buttery inside, and the white wine cream sauce is full of luscious flavor.

2 tablespoons olive oil

1½ pounds bay scallops

Table salt

Freshly ground black pepper

1 pound fettuccini or other long pasta

3 garlic cloves, minced

1 tablespoon butter

¼ cup dry white wine

¾ cup heavy (whipping) cream

2 tablespoons chopped fresh parsley

1. In a large sauté pan or skillet over medium heat, heat the olive oil. Add the scallops and sear both sides for several minutes until a thin crust forms. Season with salt and pepper to taste. Remove from the pan and set aside.

2. Meanwhile, in a 6-quart pot over high heat, bring 4 quarts of salted water to a boil. Add the pasta, stir, and cook for about 2 minutes less than the box instructs to just under al dente.

3. Return the sauté pan to medium heat and add the garlic and butter to melt, stirring to scrape up any browned bits from the bottom of the pan. Add the white wine and let reduce for 2 to 3 minutes. Stir in the heavy cream and simmer for 3 to 4 minutes.

4. Drain the pasta and add it to the sauce, mixing well to coat. Add the scallops and parsley. Serve immediately while hot.

Cooking tip: Pay close attention to the sauce once you have added the cream so it doesn't curdle. Mix well and reduce the heat, if needed.

LINGUINI WITH LEMONY COD

Serves 4

Prep time: 10 minutes **/ Cook time:** 20 minutes

5-Ingredient / 30 Minutes or Less

This lemony dish is a super light recipe ideal for anyone watching their calorie intake. It's also adaptable to every seafood you can think of, such as salmon, swordfish, flounder, and halibut; adjust your cooking time accordingly.

Table salt

1 pound linguini or other long pasta

2 tablespoons olive oil

2 garlic cloves, diced

1 pound cod loins, cut into 4-inch pieces

Juice of 2 lemons

½ cup water

Freshly ground black pepper

2 tablespoons chopped fresh parsley, plus more for garnish

2 teaspoons dried oregano

1. In a 6-quart pot over high heat, bring 4 quarts of salted water to a boil. Add the pasta, stir, and cook for about 2 minutes less than the box instructs to just under al dente.

2. Meanwhile, in a large sauté pan or skillet over medium heat, heat the olive oil. Stir in the garlic. Add the cod and sauté for 3 to 4 minutes.

3. Add the lemon juice and water and season with salt and pepper to taste. Stir in the parsley and oregano. Cover the pan and cook for 12 to 14 minutes until the fish is cooked through, depending on its thickness.

4. Drain the pasta and add it to the sauté pan. Gently toss all the ingredients, being careful not to break the fish. Transfer into individual serving bowls with several spoons of the light sauce and top with more parsley.

ANOTHER PASTABILITY

Linguini in Broth: Swap the lemon juice for water (about ¼ cup). Add several halved cherry tomatoes to the sauce, during step 3. The resulting sauce is light, fragrant, and delicate.

QUICK CIOPPINO

Serves 6

Prep time: 15 minutes **/ Cook time:** 35 minutes

Worth the Wait

The original Cioppino recipe comes from San Francisco. Italian and Portuguese fishermen would take the day's catch and turn it into a tomato-based fish stew or soup. This recipe uses only a few varieties of seafood to make it more convenient and economical. The addition of small-cut pasta makes it more satiating.

¼ cup olive oil

1 onion, diced

4 garlic cloves, minced

2 tablespoons chopped fresh parsley

1 teaspoon dried oregano

Table salt

Freshly ground black pepper

1 (14.5-ounce) can crushed tomatoes

2 cups water

1 cup dry white wine

8 ounces ditalini, shells, elbows, or other small-cut pasta

1 pound cod loins, cut into 2-inch pieces

8 ounces to 1 pound bay scallops

8 ounces large shrimp, peeled and deveined

1. In a large stockpot over medium heat, heat the olive oil. Add the onion, garlic, parsley, and oregano. Cook for 2 to 3 minutes until the onion is translucent. Season with salt and pepper to taste. Add the tomatoes, water, and white wine. Turn the heat to medium-low and simmer for 15 minutes.

2. Meanwhile, in a 5-quart pot over high heat, bring 3 quarts of salted water to a boil. Add the pasta, stir, and cook for about 2 minutes less than the box instructs to just under al dente.

3. Add the cod and scallops to the stockpot and cook for 10 to 12 minutes. Add the shrimp and cook for 3 to 4 minutes more until the seafood is cooked through.

4. Drain the pasta and add it to the stew. Simmer for 2 to 3 minutes. Serve hot.

Pair it: Serve the Citrusy Fennel Salad (page 134) as an antipasto to this stew.

RIGATONI WITH SWORDFISH AND TOMATOES

Serves 6

Prep time: 15 minutes / **Cook time:** 25 minutes

Swordfish is a personal favorite, and I am always looking for new ways to cook it. This accompanying sauce is thick, vibrant, and hearty. It's wonderful year-round, but I love it in winter, served with a nice crusty bread to mop up the leftover sauce on the plate.

3 tablespoons olive oil

3 garlic cloves, minced

6 anchovy fillets, chopped

1 tablespoon chopped fresh parsley

1 tablespoon chopped fresh basil

1 teaspoon salt, plus more for the pasta water

Freshly ground black pepper

1 pound fresh swordfish, cut into 1-inch cubes

1 (28-ounce) can crushed tomatoes

½ cup water

1 pound rigatoni

1. In a large sauté pan or skillet over medium heat, heat the olive oil. Add the garlic, anchovies, parsley, basil, and salt. Mix well, paying close attention to not burning the garlic. Season with pepper to taste and add the swordfish. Cook for 1 to 2 minutes per side to gently brown the fish.

2. Add the tomatoes and water. Increase the heat to medium and partially cover the pan with a lid. Cook for 15 to 20 minutes, stirring occasionally.

3. Meanwhile, in a 6-quart pot over high heat, bring 4 quarts of salted water to a boil. Add the pasta, stir, and cook for about 2 minutes less than the box instructs to just under al dente.

4. Reserve ¼ cup of pasta water, drain the pasta, and add it and the pasta water to the sauce. Gently mix all the ingredients. Plate and serve immediately while hot.

ANOTHER PASTABILITY

Rigatoni with Cod Loins and Tomatoes: This same recipe works wonderfully with cod loins. Cook the sauce for just 15 minutes. Cod loins are more delicate, so stir gently as they cook.

PENNE WITH SALMON, CAPERS, AND OLIVES

Serves 4

Prep time: 10 minutes **/ Cook time:** 20 minutes

30 Minutes or Less

Adaptable, versatile, and one of the healthiest fishes widely available, salmon is exceptionally tasty even when plainly prepared. However, with a few added ingredients, it can be elevated to new levels. Capers and olives are exceptionally complementary to any seafood dish, and this one is topped with a cream sauce.

3 tablespoons olive oil, divided

1 pound salmon fillets, skin removed

Table salt

1 pound penne

3 garlic cloves, minced

1 tablespoon grated lemon zest

2 tablespoons capers, drained and rinsed

¼ cup black or green olives, pitted and quartered

½ cup dry white wine

½ cup heavy (whipping) cream

Freshly ground black pepper

1. In a large sauté pan or skillet over medium heat, heat 2 tablespoons of olive oil. Add the salmon fillets and cook for 6 to 7 minutes. Turn the fish over and cook for 3 to 4 minutes on the other side. Remove the fish from the pan and set aside.

2. Meanwhile, in a 6-quart pot over high heat, bring 4 quarts of salted water to a boil. Add the pasta, stir, and cook for about 2 minutes less than the box instructs to just under al dente.

3. Return the sauté pan to medium heat and add the remaining 1 tablespoon of olive oil, the garlic, lemon zest, capers, and olives. Cook, stirring, for 1 minute, scraping up any browned bits from the bottom of the pan. Add the white wine and cook for 2 minutes to let the alcohol cook off. Stir in the heavy cream, season with salt and pepper to taste, and cook for 2 to 3 minutes.

4. Drain the pasta and add it to the pan, mix well, and cook for 1 to 2 minutes more.

5. Flake off about half the salmon and add it to the pasta, gently mixing it in. Plate the pasta in a large serving bowl and flake the remaining salmon over the top. Serve immediately while hot.

> **Cooking tip:** Avoid turning the fish more than once, as it might flake and break. To check for doneness, insert a paring knife into the thickest part of the fish to check inside. Cooked salmon will be opaque and flaky.

ANOTHER PASTABILITY

Penne with Swordfish, Capers, and Olives: If you prefer swordfish, use it instead of salmon. It will take about the same amount of time to cook.

CHAPTER FIVE

MEAT AND POULTRY

Make your pasta dishes even more tasty and satiating by combining them with meat, poultry, or sausage. Some sauces require the addition of crushed tomatoes, whereas others can be made without tomatoes. Meatless pasta dishes are often served as first courses, but adding meat to the pasta creates a combined first and second course all in one. You'll find that prep and cooking times are not much longer than when not using meats and the resulting dishes are savory and satisfying.

93

FUSILLI WITH ROASTED CHERRY TOMATOES AND CHICKEN SAUSAGES

Serves 4
Prep time: 10 minutes / **Cook time:** 30 minutes
5-Ingredient

Who doesn't love the flavors of roasted tomatoes, along with basil, extra-virgin olive oil, and oregano? These classic flavors are most often found in Italian summer salads, but they make great condiments for pasta as well. In this dish, the sauce is prepared in the oven, bringing out the best flavor from the tomatoes. Using precooked sausages means this dish comes together quickly.

2 pints cherry tomatoes, halved

1 pound pre-cooked chicken sausages, cut into 5 or 6 pieces

¼ cup olive oil

2 tablespoons chopped fresh basil

1 teaspoon dried oregano

½ teaspoon salt, plus more for the pasta water

Freshly ground black pepper

1 pound fusilli

1. Preheat the oven to 375°F. In a large bowl, toss together the tomatoes, sausages, olive oil, basil, oregano, salt, and pepper to taste until well combined. Spread everything on a baking sheet in a single layer.

2. Bake for 20 minutes, tossing occasionally.

3. Meanwhile, in a 6-quart pot over high heat, bring 4 quarts of salted water to a boil. Add the pasta, stir, and cook according to the box instructions to al dente.

4. Reserve ½ cup of pasta water and drain the pasta. Return the pasta to the pot and add the roasted tomatoes, sausages, and any juices on the baking sheet. Add a few tablespoons of pasta water and toss to combine. Serve immediately while hot.

Cooking tip: This mixture can also be prepared on the stovetop. In a large sauté pan or skillet over medium heat, heat the olive oil. Add the tomatoes, sausages, basil, oregano, salt, and pepper and cook for 20 minutes, stirring occasionally.

ANOTHER PASTABILITY

Fusilli with Roasted Cherry Tomatoes and Chicken: Follow the recipe as directed, but swap the chicken sausages for chicken tenderloins cut into 1-inch pieces. Bake for 30 minutes, then mix with the pasta.

PESTO PASTA SALAD WITH CHICKEN

Serves 4 to 6

Prep time: 10 minutes / **Cook time:** 20 minutes

Who doesn't enjoy a delicious pasta salad on a hot summer day? Ideal for picnics and beach days, pasta salads are also the perfect accompaniments to barbecues and outdoor get-togethers. Although most pasta dishes are served immediately after preparation while hot and steamy, pasta salads are great at room temperature and even cold.

4 thin chicken breast cutlets, pounded to ⅛-inch thickness

Table salt

Freshly ground black pepper

5 tablespoons extra-virgin olive oil, divided, plus more as needed

2 cups fresh basil leaves

2 garlic cloves, peeled

¼ cup pine nuts

¼ cup freshly grated Parmesan cheese

1 pound rotini, fusilli, farfalle, or other pasta of choice

1 pint cherry tomatoes, halved

1 (12-ounce) bag fresh baby spinach

1. Season the chicken breasts with salt and pepper to taste. In a large skillet over medium-high heat, heat 2 tablespoons of olive oil. Add the chicken and fry for 3 to 4 minutes per side until fully cooked. Cut the chicken into strips and set aside.

2. In a food processor, combine the basil, garlic, and 2 tablespoons of olive oil. Pulse for 1 to 2 minutes, stopping to press down the basil leaves.

3. Add the pine nuts and the remaining 1 tablespoon of olive oil. Continue pulsing for 1 to 2 minutes until a paste begins to form and the pine nuts are fully ground. Add the Parmesan cheese and pulse for about 1 minute more until a creamy paste forms.

4. Meanwhile, in a 6-quart pot over high heat, bring 4 quarts of salted water to a boil. Add the pasta, stir, and cook according to the box instructions to al dente. Reserve a few tablespoons of pasta water, drain the pasta, and transfer the pasta to a large salad bowl.

5. Add the chicken, pesto, cherry tomatoes, and spinach to the pasta bowl. Toss everything until combined. Add a few tablespoons of pasta water or olive oil to loosen the salad, if desired. Serve warm or cold.

Prep tip: Cook the chicken in the morning, refrigerate it, and prepare the rest of the dish when you come home from work.

ANOTHER PASTABILITY

Pesto Pasta Salad with Artichokes: As an alternative to spinach, add 1 (6-ounce) jar of chopped marinated artichoke hearts to the salad during the final step.

ANTIPASTO PASTA SALAD

Serves 6 to 8

Prep time: 15 minutes / **Cook time:** 15 minutes

30 Minutes or Less

Everyone loves this pasta dish because it's delicious and vibrant and requires very little cooking. This dish is less about precision and all about assembling delicious, high-quality ingredients. Get creative with other add-ins such as pickled vegetables, provolone cheese, diced pancetta, sliced prosciutto, mortadella cubes, pickled peperoncini, and raw bell peppers.

¼ cup extra-virgin olive oil

3 tablespoons red wine vinegar or balsamic vinegar

1 teaspoon dried oregano

½ teaspoon salt, plus more for the pasta water

Freshly ground black pepper

1 pound rotini, fusilli, gemelli, or other pasta of choice

1 (12-ounce) jar artichoke hearts, drained and chopped

1 (12-ounce) jar roasted red peppers, drained and cut into ¼-inch strips

1 (8-ounce) mozzarella cheese ball, cut into ½-inch cubes

5 ounces sliced salami or sopressata, cut into ½-inch strips

1 cup olives, pitted and halved

½ red onion, chopped

1. In a small bowl, whisk the olive oil, vinegar, oregano, salt, and pepper to taste until the dressing is combined. Set aside.

2. In a 6-quart pot over high heat, bring 4 quarts of salted water to a boil. Add the pasta, stir, and cook according to the box instructions to al dente. Drain and transfer the pasta to a large salad bowl.

3. Add the dressing to the pasta and mix well to coat.

4. Add the artichoke hearts, roasted red peppers, mozzarella, salami, olives, and red onion. Toss to combine. Serve at room temperature or cold. Refrigerate and enjoy within 24 hours.

CHICKEN, ZITI, AND BROCCOLI

Serves 4 to 6

Prep time: 10 minutes / **Cook time:** 20 minutes

30 Minutes or Less

This Italian American staple seems to find its way onto every Italian restaurant menu. It can be made with creamy sauces (see *Another Pastability*), olive oil, or a combination of oil and butter. Mix it up and find your own favorite version!

⅓ cup olive oil

1 onion, diced

2 garlic cloves, minced

1 tablespoon chopped fresh parsley

1 teaspoon salt, plus more for the pasta water

4 (4- to 5-ounce) boneless, skinless chicken breasts, cut into 1-inch pieces

1 pound ziti

1 pound broccoli florets

Freshly grated Parmesan cheese, for serving (optional)

1. In a very large sauté pan or skillet over medium heat, heat the olive oil. Add the onion and garlic and cook for 3 to 4 minutes. Stir in the parsley and salt.

2. Add the chicken and sauté for 12 to 14 minutes until almost fully cooked.

3. Meanwhile, in a 6-quart pot over high heat, bring 4 quarts of salted water to a boil. Add the pasta, stir, and cook for 4 minutes. Add the broccoli florets to the pasta. Continue cooking for about 5 more minutes until the pasta is al dente and the florets are crisp-tender.

4. Reserve ¼ cup of pasta water, drain the pasta and broccoli, and add them to the sauté pan with the chicken. Toss well to combine and cook for 2 minutes. Top with the Parmesan cheese (if using), and serve hot or at room temperature.

ANOTHER PASTABILITY

Chicken, Ziti, and Broccoli in Creamy White Sauce: Add 1 cup béchamel sauce (see Pasta with Béchamel Sauce, page 32) at the end of step 4 for a creamy alternative.

ORECCHIETTE WITH CHICKEN AND SWEET RED PEPPERS

Serves 4 to 6

Prep time: 15 minutes / **Cook time:** 25 minutes

Orecchiette means "little ears" in Italian, and the name matches their shape. It's used most often in southern Italy. I love this shape in sauces that call for sautéed sausage, chicken, or turkey. It's also small enough to add to soups.

¼ cup olive oil, plus more as needed

1 small onion, diced

2 garlic cloves, minced

2 tablespoons dried oregano

3 or 4 (4- to 5-ounce) boneless, skinless chicken breasts, cut into 1-inch pieces

2 red bell peppers, cut into ½-inch strips

½ teaspoon salt, plus more for the pasta water

Freshly ground black pepper

1 pound orecchiette pasta

1. In a large sauté pan or skillet over medium heat, heat the olive oil. Add the onion, garlic, and oregano. Cook for 1 to 2 minutes.

2. Add the chicken, and sauté for 3 to 4 minutes, mixing with a wooden spoon. Add the red bell peppers, season with salt and pepper to taste, and reduce the heat to low. Cook for about 15 minutes until the chicken is cooked through. If the oil dries up too quickly or the peppers stick to the pan, add more oil or several tablespoons of pasta water.

3. Meanwhile, in a 6-quart pot over high heat, bring 4 quarts of salted water to a boil. Add the pasta, stir, and cook for about 2 minutes less than the box instructs to just under al dente.

4. Reserve ¼ cup of pasta water and drain the orecchiette. Add the pasta to the sauté pan and cook for 2 to 3 minutes, mixing well. Add the reserved pasta water, if needed. Serve hot or at room temperature.

ANOTHER PASTABILITY

Orecchiette with Sausage and Sweet Red Peppers: Swap the chicken for sausage for the classic sausage and peppers combination.

GEMELLI WITH MUSHROOMS AND CHICKEN IN CREAM SAUCE

Serves 4 to 6

Prep time: 10 minutes / **Cook time:** 30 minutes

Heavy cream and half-and-half are wonderful ingredients to keep in the fridge for savory, creamy sauces enjoyed by adults and kids alike. This recipe is perfect for those chilly nights when you need something satisfying and filling.

5 tablespoons olive oil, divided

1 large onion, cut into slices

½ teaspoon salt, plus more for the pasta water

Freshly ground black pepper

3 large portabella mushrooms, diced or sliced

12 chicken tenders (tenderloins), diced

1 pound gemelli

1 cup heavy cream

Freshly grated Parmesan cheese, for serving (optional)

1. In a large sauté pan or skillet over medium-low heat, heat 3 tablespoons of oil. Add the onion and season with the salt and pepper to taste. Cook for at least 10 minutes, or more, until caramelized.

2. Add the mushrooms and cook for about 5 minutes until fully cooked. Remove the onions and mushrooms from the pan and set aside.

3. Add the remaining 2 tablespoons of olive oil and the chicken tenders to the pan and cook for 8 to 9 minutes until fully cooked and browned on all sides.

4. Meanwhile, in a 6-quart pot over high heat, bring 4 quarts of salted water to a boil. Add the pasta, stir, and cook for about 2 minutes less than the box instructs to just under al dente.

5. Add the onions and mushrooms to the chicken, along with the heavy cream. Stir the ingredients to combine, scraping up any browned bits from the bottom of the pan, and simmer for 3 to 4 minutes until the cream thickens.

6. Drain the pasta and add it to the pan, stirring to coat everything evenly with the sauce. Serve immediately while hot, topped with the Parmesan cheese (if using).

LEMONY CHICKEN WITH SHELLS AND CHARD

Serves 4

Prep time: 15 minutes / **Cook time:** 35 minutes

Worth the Wait

I cook Swiss chard often in pasta dishes and combine it with other vegetables or legumes, such as potatoes or beans. It's healthy, easy to cook, and versatile. In this recipe, we'll pair it with some chicken and shells for a light dish that packs lots of lemony flavor.

8 ounces Swiss chard, chopped into 1-inch pieces

½ cup all-purpose flour

Table salt

Freshly ground black pepper

3 (4- to 5-ounce) boneless, skinless chicken breasts, cut into 1-inch cubes

4 tablespoons olive oil, divided

8 ounces miniature shells

1 pint cherry tomatoes, halved

3 tablespoons freshly squeezed lemon juice

1. Bring a medium pot of water to a boil over high heat. Add the Swiss chard and blanch for 3 to 4 minutes. Drain and set aside.

2. In a small bowl, combine the flour with salt and pepper to taste. Stir to combine. Coat the chicken pieces in the flour, removing any excess.

3. In a large sauté pan or skillet over medium heat, heat 3 tablespoons of olive oil. Add the chicken and sauté for 7 to 8 minutes. Remove the chicken from the pan and set aside.

4. In a 6-quart pot over high heat, bring 4 quarts of salted water to a boil. Add the pasta, stir, and cook for about 2 minutes less than the box instructs to just under al dente.

5. Meanwhile, in the same sauté pan over medium heat, heat the remaining 1 tablespoon of olive oil. Add the cherry tomatoes and lemon juice and cook for 2 to 3 minutes.

6. Stir in the Swiss chard and chicken and cook for 2 to 3 minutes until the chard is fully reheated.

7. Reserve a few tablespoons of pasta water, drain the pasta, and add the pasta to the sauté pan. Toss to combine, adding the pasta water, if needed. Cook for 1 or 2 minutes until the pasta is fully cooked. Serve hot or at room temperature.

ANOTHER PASTABILITY

Lemony Chicken with Shells and Spinach: Substitute spinach for the Swiss chard for an even quicker result and less work. The spinach does not need to be blanched as it cooks quickly and is much more tender than the chard.

ANGRY PASTA WITH CHICKEN

Serves 4 to 6

Prep time: 15 minutes / **Cook time:** 1 hour

Worth the Wait

I have been eating the "less angry" version of this dish for many years. It was one of my favorite meals growing up, even as a child. My mom would make it without the red pepper flakes almost on a weekly basis, and our family was more than happy to eat it. As I got older and started teaching Italian cooking, I adapted my mom's original recipe for more heat.

1 cup all-purpose flour

½ teaspoon salt, plus more for seasoning

Freshly ground black pepper

8 bone-in skin-on chicken thighs

¼ cup olive oil

½ small onion, diced

2 garlic cloves, minced

2 tablespoons chopped fresh parsley

1 tablespoon chopped fresh basil

Red pepper flakes, for seasoning

1 (28-ounce) can crushed tomatoes

1 cup water

1 pound penne, rigatoni, or other tubular pasta

1. In a medium bowl, stir together the flour, salt, and pepper to taste. Dredge each chicken thigh in the flour, removing the excess. Discard any leftover flour.

2. In a large sauté pan or skillet over medium heat, heat the olive oil. Place the chicken in the hot oil in a single layer and brown for 6 to 7 minutes per side. Remove the chicken from the pan. Add the onion, garlic, parsley, and basil to the pan and cook, stirring, for 1 to 2 minutes. Add the red pepper flakes to taste.

3. Return the chicken to the pan. Cover the chicken with the tomatoes, add the water, season with salt, and reduce the heat to medium-low. Cover the pan and simmer for 35 to 40 minutes, stirring occasionally.

4. Meanwhile, in a 6-quart pot over high heat, bring 4 quarts of salted water to a boil. Add the pasta, stir, and cook for about 2 minutes less than the box instructs to just under al dente.

5. When the chicken is cooked, remove it from the sauce and transfer to a warmed platter. Drain the pasta and add it to the sauce. Toss to combine and cook for 1 to 2 minutes. Spoon the pasta into individual bowls and serve hot, along with the chicken.

Cooking tip: If you want to cut 15 minutes from the cooking time in step 3, use boneless, skinless chicken thighs, which cook faster than bone-in thighs. The sauce will still be delicious and a bit lighter, too.

ANOTHER PASTABILITY

Angry Whole-Wheat Penne with Sausage: If you want to add even more heat to this dish, use hot Italian sausage instead of chicken. Also, this is a thick sauce that lends itself well to whole-wheat pasta.

FETTUCCINI WITH TURKEY MARSALA

Serves 4 to 6

Prep time: 15 minutes / **Cook time:** 35 minutes

Worth the Wait

Chicken or turkey Marsala is another classic Italian American dish that combines thin cutlets with mushrooms, stock, butter, oil, and, of course, the star of the show, Marsala wine. The beauty of this restaurant-quality dish is that it comes together very quickly and is very adaptable to the meat you choose (chicken, pork, turkey, veal), and to whatever mushrooms you have on hand (baby bella, cremini, white button). It's often paired with fettuccini or other long pasta.

½ cup all-purpose flour

½ teaspoon salt, plus more for seasoning

Freshly ground black pepper

4 to 6 turkey cutlets, pounded to ¼-inch thickness

2 tablespoons olive oil

2 tablespoons butter, divided

1 pound fettuccini

8 ounces baby bella mushrooms, sliced

2 tablespoons chopped fresh parsley

¾ cup Marsala wine

¾ cup low-sodium chicken stock

1. Place the flour in a shallow dish and season with salt and pepper to taste. Gently coat both sides of the turkey cutlets with the flour and set aside.

2. In a large sauté pan or skillet over medium heat, heat the olive oil. Add 1 tablespoon of butter to melt. Add the cutlets to the pan and fry for 5 minutes per side, working in batches if the pan is not large enough. Remove the cutlets, place them in a clean dish, and set aside. Return the pan to the heat.

3. In a 6-quart pot over high heat, bring 4 quarts of salted water to a boil. Add the pasta, stir, and cook for about 2 minutes less than the box instructs to just under al dente.

4. Meanwhile, as the pasta cooks, add the mushrooms and parsley to the pan, stirring to scrape up any browned bits from the bottom. Sauté for 5 minutes. Season with salt and pepper to taste.

5. Add the wine and chicken stock and bring to a full boil. Cook for 5 minutes until the sauce has thickened and the liquid is reduced. Stir in the remaining 1 tablespoon of butter to melt.

6. Drain the pasta and add it to the sauce. Toss to combine and finish cooking the pasta. Return the turkey to the pan and cook for 2 to 3 minutes until reheated. Plate the pasta, add 1 tablespoon of sauce to each serving, and place a cutlet on top. Serve immediately while hot.

Cooking tip: Flour is a thickening agent and will thicken any sauce. If the sauce is not thickening during step 4, add 1 teaspoon of all-purpose flour. Mix it well with a wooden spoon to dissolve it entirely.

ANOTHER PASTABILITY

Fettuccini with Chicken Marsala and Spinach: Swap the turkey for chicken and add several cups of fresh spinach near the end of step 5.

ZITI WITH WHITE TURKEY BOLOGNESE

Serves 6 to 8

Prep time: 10 minutes / **Cook time:** 40 minutes

Worth the Wait

I've been using ground turkey in my kitchen for some 20 years now and find it very adaptable and lighter than ground beef. It's wonderful in meatballs and meatloaves, as well as in various sauces. Traditional Bolognese ragù calls for ground beef and crushed tomatoes, and you will find a wonderful recipe on page 121, but try this turkey version without tomatoes and broaden your ragù repertoire.

¼ cup olive oil

½ small onion, diced

2 carrots, peeled and finely diced

1 celery stalk, finely diced

½ teaspoon salt, plus more for the pasta water

Freshly ground black pepper

1 pound lean ground turkey

1 cup dry white wine

2 cups low-sodium chicken stock

1 pound ziti

½ cup heavy (whipping) cream

Freshly grated Parmesan cheese, for serving (optional)

1. In a large sauté pan or skillet over medium heat, heat the olive oil. Add the onion, carrots, and celery. Sauté for 5 to 7 minutes. Season with salt and pepper to taste and stir to combine.

2. Add the ground turkey and use a wooden spoon to break it up. Cook for 4 to 5 minutes to brown.

3. Add the white wine and cook for 3 to 4 minutes until reduced by about half.

4. Add the chicken stock, reduce the heat to low, and simmer, uncovered, for 25 to 30 minutes, stirring occasionally.

5. Meanwhile, in a 6-quart pot over high heat, bring 4 quarts of salted water to a boil. Add the pasta, stir, and cook for about 2 minutes less than the box instructs to just under al dente.

6. As the pasta cooks, add the heavy cream to the sauce and stir, bringing the sauce back to a slight simmer.

7. Reserve a few tablespoons of pasta water and drain the pasta. Add the pasta to the sauce and toss to coat. Cook for 1 to 2 minutes more, adding the pasta water, if needed. Serve immediately while hot in individual dishes or in a large serving bowl, family style. Top with the Parmesan cheese (if using).

Cooking tip: As you've probably noticed by now, a lot of pasta dishes start with preparing the sauces, then cooking the pasta and mixing the pasta into the sauce. Make sure you're using a large enough sauté pan or skillet to accommodate adding ½ to 1 pound of cooked pasta.

SKILLET PASTA WITH TURKEY AND SPINACH

Serves 4

Prep time: 10 minutes / **Cook time:** 30 minutes

Unless I am cooking soups or stews, it's not very often that I cook the pasta directly with the sauce. That said, sometimes we're all looking to cut the cooking time and occasionally it just works. I wouldn't use an entire pound of pasta with this method, but when you're cooking just a half pound, it's the ideal one-pot pasta dish!

2 tablespoons olive oil

1 small onion, diced

2 garlic cloves, minced

1 pound ground turkey

1 teaspoon salt

Freshly ground black pepper

1 (14.5-ounce) can crushed tomatoes

4 cups low-sodium chicken broth or vegetable broth

8 ounces ziti or penne

1 (12-ounce) bag fresh baby spinach

½ cup shredded mozzarella cheese

1. In a large saucepan over medium heat, heat the olive oil. Add the onion and cook for 2 to 3 minutes. Add the garlic and cook, stirring, for just 1 minute or so. Add the ground turkey and use a wooden spoon to break it up. Add salt and season with pepper to taste. Cook for 7 to 8 minutes, stirring occasionally.

2. Add the tomatoes and chicken broth. Cook for 5 minutes, stirring occasionally.

3. Add the dried pasta to the saucepan and cook for about 7 minutes.

4. Add the spinach, pressing it down using the wooden spoon. Cook for about 3 minutes until the pasta is al dente.

5. Remove from the heat and stir in the mozzarella cheese, mixing well until the cheese melts. Serve immediately while hot.

> **Cooking tip:** Use simple pasta shapes with this cooking method. Anything with too many ridges or details, such as gemelli or rotini, takes longer to cook and requires more broth. Also, whole-wheat pasta does not work well using this method.

ANOTHER PASTABILITY

Skillet Pasta with Sausage and Swiss Chard: For a variation on this dish, substitute sausage (removed from its casing) for the ground turkey and Swiss chard for the spinach.

LENTIL AND PASTA SOUP WITH SPINACH AND SAUSAGE

Serves 4 to 6

Prep time: 15 minutes, plus overnight to soak the lentils / **Cook time:** 45 minutes

Worth the Wait

There is something so comforting about lentil soup, and nothing compares to it. I eat it often during winter months, but I always make sure to enjoy a big bowl on New Year's Day. Italian tradition says lentils resemble coins and thus, to guarantee a prosperous New Year, everyone should enjoy a hearty dish of lentils. You can use low-sodium vegetable stock in place of the vegetable bouillon cube. Simply replace the water with the stock.

1 cup dried lentils

3 tablespoons olive oil

1 small onion, finely diced

2 tablespoons chopped fresh parsley

2 carrots, peeled and diced

1 celery stalk, diced

1 teaspoon salt

3 or 4 pork sausages, thinly sliced

1 cup canned tomato sauce or canned crushed tomatoes

½ large vegetable bouillon cube

8 ounces elbows, ditalini, or miniature shells

1 (12-ounce) bag fresh spinach

1. In a large bowl, combine the lentils with enough cold water to cover. Let soak overnight. Drain and rinse. Set aside.

2. In a 6-quart soup pot over medium heat, heat the olive oil. Add the onion, parsley, carrots, celery, and salt. Sauté for 2 to 3 minutes.

3. Add the sausages and brown for about 2 minutes. Stir in the tomato sauce and simmer for 1 minute.

4. Add the lentils and plenty of water, filling the pan almost to the top, leaving a few inches of space. Bring to a full boil and add the vegetable bouillon cube. Simmer over medium heat for 20 minutes.

5. Add the pasta and cook for 8 to 10 minutes. During the last few minutes, add the spinach, pressing down with a wooden spoon to wilt. Serve hot.

BOWTIES WITH PEAS, MUSHROOMS, AND SAUSAGE

Serves 4

Prep time: 15 minutes / **Cook time:** 30 minutes

I remember being in grade school the first time I had this dish. My elementary school in Italy was directly across the street from our home, and I would often look out the window and daydream about what my mom was preparing for when we were dismissed from school! I came home one day and this was waiting for my sister and me. School let out at 12:30, so she always had something delicious waiting for us all to enjoy for lunch at the end of our school day.

¼ cup olive oil, plus more for drizzling

1 small onion, diced

1 or 2 tablespoons chopped fresh parsley

6 sausages (pork or chicken, hot or sweet), cut into 5 or 6 pieces each

1 (12-ounce) bag frozen peas

2 cups water

½ teaspoon salt, plus more for the pasta water

8 ounces white button mushrooms, sliced

1 pound farfalle

Freshly grated Parmesan cheese, for serving (optional)

1. In a large sauté pan or skillet over medium heat, heat the olive oil. Add the onion and parsley and cook for 2 to 3 minutes. Add the sausage pieces and cook for 2 to 3 minutes, turning, until browned on all sides.

2. Add the peas and water, season with salt, and cook for 15 minutes, uncovered, stirring occasionally.

3. Meanwhile, in a 6-quart pot over high heat, bring 4 quarts of salted water to a boil. Add the pasta, stir, and cook for about 2 minutes less than the box instructs to just under al dente.

4. After the peas have cooked for 15 minutes, add the mushrooms. Cook for 5 to 6 minutes more, stirring occasionally.

continued

5. Drain the pasta and add it to the sauté pan. Toss to combine and cook for 1 minute until the pasta is fully cooked. Serve in a large serving bowl, family style. Drizzle with olive oil and top with the Parmesan cheese (if using). Serve immediately while hot.

Cooking tip: It's much easier to slice sausages if they are placed in the freezer for 30 to 60 minutes before needed.

ANOTHER PASTABILITY

Orecchiette with Peas, Artichokes, and Chicken: Orecchiette is a nice cut of pasta to use with any dish containing peas. Swap the mushrooms for frozen artichoke hearts and the sausage for diced chicken breast for a completely different dish.

GNOCCHI WITH SAUSAGE RAGÙ

Serves 6 to 8

Prep time: 10 minutes / **Cook time:** 1 hour

Worth the Wait

Gnocchi with sausage is a wonderful combination enjoyed throughout Italy, but it's especially loved in the south. This comfort food is traditionally enjoyed in winter months, when cravings turn to something more satisfying. This dish takes a few extra minutes to prepare, but the prep time is minimal and the stove does much of the work for you.

¼ cup olive oil

2 carrots, peeled and diced

2 celery stalks, diced

1 small onion, diced

6 to 8 Italian sausages, casings removed

1 teaspoon salt, plus more for the gnocchi water

Freshly ground black pepper

1 cup red wine

1 (28-ounce) can canned crushed tomatoes

1 pound shelf-stable gnocchi

1. In a large sauté pan or skillet over medium heat, heat the olive oil. Add the carrots, celery, and onion. Sauté for 5 to 6 minutes.

2. Add the sausage and use a wooden spoon to break it up to resemble ground meat. Add the salt and season with pepper to taste. Stir in the red wine and cook for 2 to 3 minutes.

3. Add the tomatoes, reduce the heat to medium-low, and cook, uncovered, for 40 to 45 minutes, stirring occasionally.

4. Meanwhile, in a 6-quart pot over high heat, bring 4 quarts of salted water to a boil. Add the gnocchi, stir, and cook for 1 minute less than the package instructs.

continued

5. Drain the gnocchi and add them to the sauté pan. Stir to coat with the sauce and cook for 1 minute. Serve immediately while hot.

Substitution tip: This is a sturdy, hearty sauce, so feel free to substitute whole-wheat pasta in this recipe.

ANOTHER PASTABILITY

Baked Ziti with Sausage Ragù: Follow the recipe as directed, but substitute ziti for the gnocchi. Place everything in a buttered baking dish, top with shredded mozzarella cheese, and bake in a 375°F oven for 15 minutes until heated through and the cheese melts.

GEMELLI WITH SUN-DRIED TOMATOES, ASPARAGUS, AND PROSCIUTTO

Serves 4 to 6

Prep time: 10 minutes / **Cook time:** 25 minutes

5-Ingredient

Prosciutto-wrapped asparagus is served as an appetizer throughout Italy and in many Italian American homes in the United States. In this recipe, I pair the two ingredients instead to form a delicious pasta dish. The added sun-dried tomatoes pack a flavor punch, and with the fun gemelli shapes, you have a wonderful dinner. This recipe makes terrific leftovers—just reheat in the microwave for a few minutes.

1 pound asparagus, woody ends removed, halved

4 ounces prosciutto, cut into ½-inch strips, or pancetta, cubed

½ teaspoon salt, plus more for the pasta water

1 pound gemelli

2 tablespoons olive oil

1 garlic clove, minced

3 or 4 ounces oil-packed sun-dried tomatoes, chopped, oil reserved

Freshly ground black pepper

1. Bring a medium pot of water to a boil over high heat. Add the asparagus and blanch for 5 to 8 minutes, or according to your preference for doneness. Drain.

2. In a small sauté pan or skillet over medium heat, cook the prosciutto for 2 to 3 minutes until crispy. Remove from the pan and set aside.

3. In a 6-quart pot over high heat, bring 4 quarts of salted water to a boil. Add the pasta, stir, and cook for about 2 minutes less than the box instructs to just under al dente.

continued

4. Meanwhile, as the pasta cooks, in a large sauté pan or skillet over medium heat, heat the olive oil. Add the blanched asparagus, garlic, and sun-dried tomatoes with their oil. Sauté for 3 to 4 minutes. Add the prosciutto to the pan and toss to combine.

5. Reserve 1 cup of pasta water, drain the pasta, and add the pasta to the sauté pan, mixing well to coat. Add the reserved pasta water and finish cooking the pasta for 2 minutes more. Season with pepper to taste and serve immediately while hot.

Substitution tip: To make this dish vegetarian, swap sliced mushrooms for the prosciutto.

PAPPARDELLE WITH PROSCIUTTO AND MUSHROOMS

Serves 4 to 6

Prep time: 10 minutes / **Cook time:** 20 minutes

30 Minutes or Less

Mushrooms and prosciutto? What's not to love? This pasta is one of my favorite go-tos because it's super quick and flavorful, and I pretty much love anything involving prosciutto. The longest part is waiting for the pasta water to boil. Pappardelle is the cut of pasta typically used in this dish, but you could swap it for anything else. Use salt judiciously when cooking with prosciutto; as it's salt-cured, it already adds sodium to your dishes.

Table salt

1 pound pappardelle

¼ cup olive oil

2 garlic cloves, minced

1 rosemary sprig, leaves removed and chopped

1 pound cremini, portabella, or shiitake mushrooms, or a combination, sliced

Freshly ground black pepper

½ cup red wine

½ pound thickly sliced prosciutto, chopped into ¼-inch dice

Freshly grated Parmesan cheese, for serving (optional)

1. In a 6-quart pot over high heat, bring 4 quarts of salted water to a boil. Add the pasta, stir, and cook for about 2 minutes less than the box instructs to just under al dente.

2. Meanwhile, as the pasta cooks, in a large sauté pan or skillet over medium heat, heat the olive oil. Add the garlic and rosemary and sauté for 1 minute.

3. Add the mushrooms and season with salt and pepper to taste. Sauté for 1 to 2 minutes.

4. Reduce the heat to low, add the red wine, and cook, uncovered, for 6 to 7 minutes, stirring occasionally. Add the prosciutto and cook for 1 to 2 minutes more.

continued

5. Reserve a few tablespoons of pasta water, drain the pasta, and add the pasta to the sauté pan. Toss to combine and cook for 2 minutes, adding the pasta water if the sauce is dry. Plate and serve immediately while hot. Top with the Parmesan cheese (if using).

Cooking tip: Authentic Italian prosciutto is always best sliced thinly when eaten in panini, but when used in cooking, ask for it thickly cut, as it will be much easier to dice.

ANOTHER PASTABILITY

Pappardelle with Prosciutto and Mushrooms in Cream Sauce: For a creamy sauce, follow the recipe as directed and add ½ cup heavy (whipping) cream right before adding the pasta to the sauté pan.

EASIER TAGLIATELLE AL RAGÙ

Serves 4 to 6

Prep time: 10 minutes / **Cook time:** 40 minutes

Worth the Wait

Many believe that to get the best ragù, you must cook it for hours on end. The reality is that ground meat just doesn't take that long to cook and shouldn't require that many hours on the stove. This easier version comes together quickly, and then the stove does the rest of the work. With only occasional stirring, there's no reason to wait for the weekend for this hearty dish.

¼ cup olive oil

1 carrot, peeled and finely diced

1 celery stalk, finely diced

1 small onion, finely diced

4 ounces deli-style pancetta, diced

1 pound lean ground beef

½ teaspoon salt, plus more for the pasta water

Freshly ground black pepper

½ cup red wine or beef broth

1 (28-ounce) can crushed tomatoes

1 pound tagliatelle

¾ cup whole milk

Freshly grated Parmesan cheese, for serving (optional)

1. In a large sauté pan or skillet over medium heat, heat the olive oil. Add the carrot, celery, onion, and pancetta. Sauté for 2 minutes.

2. Add the ground beef and break it up with a wooden spoon. Add ½ teaspoon of salt and season with pepper to taste. Sauté for 7 to 8 minutes.

3. Add the red wine and cook for 3 to 4 minutes, letting it reduce. Stir in the tomatoes and cook for about 25 minutes, uncovered, stirring occasionally.

4. Meanwhile, in a 6-quart pot over high heat, bring 4 quarts of salted water to a boil. Add the pasta, stir, and cook for about 2 minutes less than the box instructs to just under al dente.

continued

5. As the pasta cooks, add the milk to the sauce, stir, and cook for 5 to 6 minutes more. Reserve about 2 cups of sauce and set it aside.

6. Reserve a few tablespoons of pasta water, drain the pasta, and add the pasta to the sauce in the pan, tossing to combine. Add the pasta water, if needed. Divide the pasta into individual dishes and top with an additional spoonful or two of the reserved sauce. Top with Parmesan cheese (if using).

Substitution tip: Elevate this dish to special occasion status by using fresh tagliatelle or fettuccini.

EASIER WEEKNIGHT LASAGNA

Serves 6 to 8

Prep time: 20 minutes **/ Cook time:** 1 hour 15 minutes

Worth the Wait

If there is one dish everyone recognizes as Italian, it is lasagna. Layered pasta with sauce, cheese, and sausage is the classic combination, but these days, there are countless styles including vegetarian, as well as some using various vegetable slices in place of the pasta sheets. This version is simplified to make it more attainable during the week.

3 tablespoons olive oil

6 pork sausages, hot or sweet, casings removed

½ small onion, chopped

4 tablespoons chopped fresh parsley, divided

2 garlic cloves, minced

1½ teaspoon salt, divided

1 (16-ounce) container whole-milk ricotta

2 cups shredded mozzarella cheese, divided

2 large eggs, slightly beaten

1 cup freshly grated Parmesan cheese, divided

Nonstick cooking spray

4 cups homemade tomato sauce (see Pasta al Pomodoro, page 25), divided

1 (9-ounce) box no-cook lasagna sheets

1. In a medium sauté pan or skillet over medium-high heat, heat 3 tablespoons of olive oil. Add the sausages and break them up with a wooden spoon until they resemble ground meat. Add the onion, 2 tablespoons of parsley, the garlic, and ½ teaspoon of salt. Sauté for 15 minutes and set aside.

2. In a medium bowl, using a fork, gently mix the ricotta, 1 cup of mozzarella cheese, the eggs, the remaining 2 tablespoons of parsley, ½ cup of Parmesan cheese, and the remaining 1 teaspoon of salt until just until combined; do not overmix. Set aside.

3. Preheat the oven to 375°F. Grease a 9-by-13-inch baking pan with cooking spray.

continued

4. Spread one-third of the tomato sauce over the bottom of the prepared pan. Layer 6 or 7 lasagna sheets over the sauce, side by side, overlapping slightly. Add half the ricotta mixture and spread it evenly. Add half the sausage mixture over the ricotta and spread it evenly. Sprinkle with ⅓ cup of mozzarella and one-third of the remaining Parmesan cheese.

5. Spread half the remaining sauce over the top. Layer with another 6 or 7 lasagna sheets and add the remaining ricotta mixture, spreading it evenly. Top with the remaining sausage and spread it evenly. Sprinkle with ⅓ cup of mozzarella and half the remaining Parmesan.

6. Top with the remaining sauce. Sprinkle on the remaining ⅓ cup of mozzarella and remaining Parmesan.

7. Bake, uncovered, for 50 minutes until the top is bubbly. Let the lasagna sit at room temperature for 10 to 15 minutes before slicing and serving.

Prep tip: The tomato sauce, sausage, and ricotta mixture can all be prepared in advance for ease of preparation. The sauce can be prepared up to 3 days ahead and refrigerated until ready to use. The sausage can be sautéed up to the day before and the ricotta mixture can be prepared up to 2 to 3 hours in advance.

ANOTHER PASTABILITY

Vegetarian Lasagna: For a vegetarian option, skip the sausage. It's just as satisfying without it and takes less time to prepare. Bake for 40 minutes instead of 50.

BAKED PASTA WITH GROUND BEEF AND MOZZARELLA

Serves 6 to 8

Prep time: 15 minutes / **Cook time:** 50 minutes

Worth the Wait

Ground meat is a great option for weeknight dinners because it cooks much faster than entire cuts of meat, making it a convenient choice. Using the oven, instead of stirring on the stovetop, means the oven does a lot of the work, freeing you up while dinner cooks. This dish is filled with fresh mozzarella and serves at least six people, but you can easily halve the recipe for smaller portions.

Nonstick cooking spray

3 tablespoons olive oil

1 small onion, chopped

2 or 3 garlic cloves, peeled

1½ pounds lean ground beef

Table salt

1 pound penne

½ cup canned crushed tomatoes

2 tablespoons chopped fresh parsley

¼ cup freshly grated Parmesan cheese, plus more for topping

2 large (8-ounce) mozzarella balls, cut into ½-inch cubes

1. Preheat the oven to 375°F. Coat a 9-by-13-inch baking dish with cooking spray. Set aside.

2. In a large sauté pan or skillet over medium heat, heat the olive oil. Add the onion and garlic and sauté for 2 to 3 minutes.

3. Add the ground beef and use a wooden spoon to break up the meat. Sauté for 5 minutes.

4. In a 6-quart pot over high heat, bring 4 quarts of salted water to a boil. Add the pasta, stir, and cook for 4 minutes less than the box instructs.

5. As the pasta cooks, add the tomatoes and parsley to the meat, mix well, and cook, stirring occasionally, for 10 minutes more. Remove the meat from the heat and stir in the Parmesan cheese to combine.

continued

6. Reserve ¼ cup of pasta water, drain the pasta, and add the pasta to the meat sauce. Stir to combine well, adding the pasta water 1 tablespoon at a time.

7. Add the mozzarella cubes and toss. Spread everything in the prepared baking dish and sprinkle with Parmesan cheese.

8. Bake for 30 minutes, or until a crunchy topping develops. Let rest for 5 minutes before serving.

Pair it: Peas with Prosciutto and Shallots (page 142) makes a wonderful *contorno*, or side, to this dish.

CLASSIC PASTA AL FORNO (SOUTHERN ITALIAN STYLE)

Serves 6 to 8

Prep time: 15 minutes / **Cook time:** 1 hour 10 minutes

Worth the Wait

There are countless variations to *pasta al forno*, and this version is in the classic style of southern Italy. Many other baked pastas call for a ricotta filling, but I much prefer the one with a ground meat sauce and filled with deli-style fillings. It's decadent, rich, and always a crowd-pleaser.

3 tablespoons olive oil

½ small onion, chopped

2 tablespoons chopped fresh parsley

1 pound ground beef or turkey or a combination

1 (28-ounce) can crushed tomatoes

1 teaspoon salt, plus more for the pasta water

1 cup water

1 pound ziti, penne, or rigatoni

½ cup freshly grated Parmesan cheese, divided

8 ounces shredded mozzarella cheese, divided

8 ounces deli-style ham, diced, divided

4 ounces deli-style salami or sopressata, diced, divided

4 large eggs, hard-boiled, peeled and diced, divided

1. In a large sauté pan or skillet over medium heat, heat the olive oil. Add the onion and parsley and sauté for 1 to 2 minutes. Add the ground meat and break it up using a wooden spoon. Sauté for 4 to 5 minutes.

2. Stir in the tomatoes, salt, and water. Turn the heat to medium-low and simmer, uncovered, for 30 minutes.

3. Meanwhile, in a 6-quart pot over high heat, bring 4 quarts of salted water to a boil. Add the pasta, stir, and cook 4 minutes less than the box instructs.

4. Preheat the oven to 375°F.

5. Scoop out about 1¼ cups of sauce and spread it in a 9-by-13-inch baking dish.

6. Drain the pasta and return it to the cooking pot. With the heat off, add 2 to 3 cups of sauce to the pasta and mix well. Reserving some of each ingredient for toppings, add almost all of the following ingredients to the pasta: Parmesan and mozzarella cheeses, ham, salami, and eggs. Mix well to combine.

7. Transfer the pasta mixture into the prepared baking dish, smoothing everything with a wooden spoon or spatula. Evenly spread the remaining sauce over the pasta. Top with the remaining Parmesan and mozzarella cheeses, ham, salami, and eggs.

8. Bake for 20 to 30 minutes, or until the topping gets crunchy. Serve hot or at room temperature.

Prep tip: The sauce can be prepared up to 2 days in advance and refrigerated until you're ready to use it. Prepare the sauce on a Sunday when, perhaps, you have more time and bake the pasta on a random Tuesday night for an elegant weeknight meal. Leftovers reheat wonderfully the next day.

ANOTHER PASTABILITY

Lighter and Quicker Pasta al Forno: For a quicker, lighter alternative, use a simple tomato sauce (see Pasta al Pomodoro, page 25) instead of this meat-based sauce.

CHAPTER SIX

SALADS, SIDES, AND DRINKS

Because we can't live on pasta alone, in this chapter you will find inventive dishes that pair wonderfully with the pasta recipes in this book. When selecting accompaniments to include here, I chose recipes that aren't overly filling because they will accompany the main course, not take it over. You want the accompaniments to whet the appetite and keep your family and guests wanting more and guessing what's next. The drinks at the end of the chapter go nicely both during dinner—and while preparing it.

ARUGULA AND RADICCHIO SALAD

Serves 4 to 6

Prep time: 15 minutes

Radicchio, in my opinion, is the unsung hero of the salad family. It's part of the cabbage family and its tangy, bitter flavor sometimes makes it a second or third choice to other more widely used salad greens. It's more popular in Italy than the United States and I urge you to try it. Because of its intense flavor profile, it goes wonderfully with strong cheeses, but also with sweet fruits, such as citrus or pear.

¼ cup extra-virgin olive oil

2 tablespoons red wine vinegar

1 tablespoon honey

1 tablespoon freshly squeezed lemon juice

Table salt

Freshly ground black pepper

2 small heads radicchio, chopped into 1-inch pieces

2 cups baby arugula

¼ cup golden raisins

1 (2-ounce) chunk Parmesan cheese

1. In a small bowl, whisk the olive oil, vinegar, honey, and lemon juice to combine. Taste and season with salt and pepper and whisk again. Set the dressing aside.

2. In a large salad bowl, combine the radicchio and arugula. Add the dressing and toss well to coat.

3. Top the salad with the raisins.

4. With a vegetable peeler, shave the Parmesan chunk over the salad. Toss gently and serve immediately.

Cooking tip: Do you find radicchio too bitter? Soaking cut radicchio in cold water for 1 hour before prepping the salad will tone down the bitterness. Dry it in a salad spinner before adding the dressing.

TOMATO SALAD WITH RED ONION, BASIL, AND OREGANO

Serves 4

Prep time: 15 minutes

5-Ingredient / 30 Minutes or Less

The simplicity of this salad can't be denied, but neither can its popularity. This summer staple in southern Italian cooking is eaten practically every night. It's great before a meal, next to a meal, or to finish a meal! The key is making sure you use juicy in-season tomatoes. If you can't find red onions, white or yellow onions will work, as will a few diced scallions.

3 vine-ripened tomatoes, diced

½ teaspoon salt

1 large English cucumber, peeled and diced

½ small red onion, diced

3 tablespoons extra-virgin olive oil

2 tablespoons chopped fresh basil

1 teaspoon dried oregano

1. In a medium bowl, combine the tomatoes and salt. If you have time, let stand for 5 to 10 minutes so the tomatoes release their juices.

2. Add the cucumber, red onion, olive oil, basil, and oregano and mix well. Serve immediately.

Cooking tip: Once the cucumber is added, serve the salad immediately. Cucumber is mostly water, and the salad will get watery if left to stand too long.

CITRUSY FENNEL SALAD

Serves 4

Prep time: 10 minutes

5-Ingredient / 30 Minutes or Less

Don't assume all salads need leafy greens! This salad is a staple in Sicilian cooking, where citrus fruits grow plentifully in the fields. Unlike many other salads, this one is ideal in winter months when oranges are at their peak. It's also very adaptable so you can substitute grapefruits for the oranges and capers or anchovies for the olives.

2 tablespoons extra-virgin olive oil

Juice of 1 lemon

½ teaspoon salt

Freshly ground black pepper

2 oranges

1 small or ½ large red onion, thinly sliced

1 fennel bulb, thinly sliced

½ cup oil-cured black olives, pitted and halved

1. In a small bowl, whisk the olive oil, lemon juice, and salt to combine. Season with pepper to taste and whisk again. Set the dressing aside.

2. Thoroughly peel the oranges and remove all the white pith. Cut the oranges into ¼-inch-thick slices and decoratively arrange the fruit on a platter. Top the oranges with the red onion slices, fennel, and olives.

3. Drizzle the dressing over the salad. Season with salt and pepper, if desired. Serve immediately.

Substitution tip: I love fennel in this salad, but if you can't find it, celery makes a wonderful, and milder, substitute. Use 5 or 6 celery stalks, thinly sliced, instead.

ESCAROLE SALAD WITH LEMON DRESSING

Serves 4

Prep time: 15 minutes

30 Minutes or Less

Growing up, I would see my dad eat escarole salad several times a week. I would tease him and call him a rabbit! I much preferred the sweetness of the Tomato Salad with Red Onion, Basil, and Oregano (page 133), and could eat that by the pound. As I got older, though, my appreciation for this bitter green grew. I now cook with it frequently and eat it in salads. Like radicchio, you can soak escarole in cold water to draw out some of its bitterness. The honey in the dressing further offsets some of the bitterness.

¼ cup extra-virgin olive oil

Juice of 2 lemons

1 tablespoon honey or maple syrup

½ teaspoon salt

Freshly ground black pepper

2 heads escarole, chopped into 1-inch pieces

½ cup black olives or green olives, pitted and halved

8 anchovy fillets, roughly chopped

¼ cup walnuts, chopped

1. In a small bowl, whisk the olive oil, lemon juice, honey, and salt to blend. Season with pepper to taste and whisk again. Set the dressing aside.

2. In a large salad bowl, combine the escarole, olives, anchovies, and walnuts.

3. Add the dressing and mix well. Serve immediately.

> **Prep tip:** The top inch or so of the escarole head is often wilted or a bit browned, so chop it off and discard it. Also, remove the outer leaves of the escarole, as they are a bit tougher and more bitter.

RICOTTA WITH HONEY CROSTINI

Serves 6 to 8

Prep time: 10 minutes / **Cook time:** 5 minutes

5-Ingredient / 30 Minutes or Less

Appetizers, or *antipasti* in Italian, are small nibbles meant to whet the appetite for what's to come as the main course. They should be delicate, enticing, and small enough so as not to spoil the main course. That said, I love these crostini so much I have been known to have them as a full meal more than once! They are like chips—you can't have just one! For a little color and an herby twist, top these crostini with some fresh thyme.

1 baguette, cut on a bias into ½-inch-thick slices

¼ cup extra-virgin olive oil

2 cups whole-milk ricotta

1 tablespoon grated citrus zest (lemon or orange or a combination)

Coarse sea salt

½ cup honey

1. Place a rack on the top shelf of the oven and preheat the broiler. If your oven doesn't have a broil setting, preheat it to the highest temperature.

2. Lightly brush both sides of the baguette slices with the olive oil. Place the bread on a baking sheet and broil for 1 to 2 minutes. Flip the bread and broil the other side for 1 to 2 minutes more. The bread should be slightly charred but not burned; keep an eye on it.

3. In a small bowl, gently whisk the ricotta and zest. Top each bread slice with 1 heaping tablespoon of the ricotta mixture. Add a light sprinkle of salt and top with a drizzle of honey. Serve immediately while hot and crisp.

Substitution tip: A great twist on these can be achieved using mascarpone cheese in place of ricotta. Mascarpone is sweeter, so it pairs wonderfully with the honey. Leave out the sea salt if you use the mascarpone. Mascarpone has the same consistency as cream cheese, so leave it at room temperature to soften for up to 1 hour before using.

GARLIC BRUSCHETTA

Serves 6 to 8

Prep time: 10 minutes **/ Cook time:** 5 minutes

5-Ingredient / 30 Minutes or Less

There are many variations to *bruschetta* (pronounced "bru-sketta" in Italian), and the basic version that goes with everything is a garlic one. Bruschetta is fun to snack on by itself, top with finely chopped tomatoes, or use as a vessel to mop up sauce or broth in soups. These cook quickly and are savory and very appetizing.

¼ cup extra-virgin olive oil

4 garlic cloves, finely minced

2 tablespoons finely chopped fresh parsley

1 teaspoon garlic powder

1 baguette, cut on a bias into ½-inch-thick slices

Coarse sea salt

Freshly ground black pepper

1. Place a rack on the top shelf of the oven and preheat the broiler. If your oven doesn't have a broil setting, preheat it to the highest temperature.

2. In a small bowl, whisk the olive oil, garlic, parsley, and garlic powder to combine. Lightly brush both sides of the baguette slices with the oil mixture. Place the bread on a baking sheet and broil for 1 to 2 minutes. Flip the bread and broil the other side for 1 to 2 minutes more. The bread should be slightly charred but not burned; keep an eye on it.

3. Remove and immediately season with salt and pepper to taste. Serve immediately while hot and crisp.

Cooking tip: For both these and the Ricotta with Honey Crostini (page 137), you want to brush the bread with olive oil very lightly. Using too much will result in soggy crostini and bruschetta.

SAUTÉED BROCCOLI RABE WITH GARLIC AND OLIVE OIL

Serves 4

Prep time: 10 minutes / **Cook time:** 15 minutes

5-Ingredient / 30 Minutes or Less

Broccoli rabe, also known as broccoli rape or *rapini* in Italian, is a wonderful fall and winter bitter green. In the south, it's most often paired with sausages and orecchiette pasta, whereas in the north, it's a common addition to soups and stews. Broccoli rabe can be bitter, but the bitterness dissipates the longer you cook it.

2 bunches broccoli rabe	3 tablespoons olive oil, plus more for drizzling	Red pepper flakes, for seasoning
Table salt	4 garlic cloves, minced	

1. Trim the broccoli rabe by removing the lower stems and outer leaves, keeping just the florets and baby leaves (see Cooking tip).

2. Bring a large pot of salted water to a boil. Add the broccoli rabe and blanch for 5 minutes. Remove from the boiling water and set aside.

3. Meanwhile, in a large sauté pan over medium heat, heat the olive oil. Add the garlic and red pepper flakes to taste. Sauté for 1 minute. Add the broccoli rabe and sauté for 2 to 3 minutes more, tossing to coat with the oil and seasoning. Serve hot, topped with a drizzle more olive oil, if desired.

Cooking tip: The florets and baby leaves from the broccoli rabe are the most tender and delicate parts. The outer leaves can be a bit bitter but are certainly edible. Reserve those for soups and stews to avoid food waste.

ROASTED VEGETABLES AU GRATIN

Serves 4 to 6

Prep time: 20 minutes / **Cook time:** 35 minutes

Worth the Wait

Vegetables au gratin is a hearty side dish that works well as an accompaniment to pastas with light sauces, such as Cacio e Pepe (page 28) and Lemony Angel Hair (page 39). The bulk of the prep is cutting the vegetables, after that, the oven does the work. The key is using a combination of water-based vegetables, such as zucchini and tomato, with low-water vegetables, such as potato.

2 tablespoons butter, diced, plus more for the baking dish

1½ cups bread crumbs, plus more for coating and topping

½ cup freshly grated Parmesan cheese, plus more for coating and topping

1 teaspoon dried oregano

½ teaspoon salt

Freshly ground black pepper

2 zucchini, cut into ½-inch circles

2 potatoes, peeled and cut into ¼-inch circles

2 tomatoes, cut into ½-inch-thick slices

2 tablespoons olive oil

1. Preheat the oven to 375°F. Generously coat a 9-by-6-inch oval baking dish with butter and coat with bread crumbs. Set aside.

2. In a medium bowl, stir together the bread crumbs, Parmesan cheese, oregano, and salt. Season with pepper to taste. Working with one vegetable at a time, dip each slice into the bread crumb mixture and coat it all over. Layer each of the coated vegetables in the prepared baking dish, placing the potato between the zucchini and tomatoes so it's in the middle of the water-based vegetables. Create a pattern from the circles or simply layer them.

3. Drizzle the vegetables with the olive oil and dot the top with 2 tablespoons of butter. Sprinkle with additional bread crumbs and Parmesan cheese.

4. Bake for 35 minutes, or until a crunchy topping forms. Serve hot straight from the oven.

Substitution tip: Eggplant is a wonderful addition or alternative in this dish. Select thinner eggplants so the slices are about the same size as the other ingredients.

STUFFED TOMATOES

Serves 4

Prep time: 20 minutes / **Cook time:** 30 minutes

5-Ingredient

One of the many joys of summer, along with beach visits, longer days, and flip-flops, is the overabundance of summer produce. One of my preferred summer vegetables (although it's actually a fruit) is tomato. Tomatoes are versatile, great raw or cooked, and a perfect accompaniment to many foods. One of my favorite ways to prepare them is stuffed. The crunchy topping is what always does me in. Once roasted, the tomatoes are juicier, sweeter, and delicious!

4 vine-ripened tomatoes or beefsteak tomatoes	½ cup freshly grated Parmesan cheese, plus more for topping	¼ cup olive oil
Table salt		2 tablespoons chopped fresh parsley
¾ cup bread crumbs	½ cup shredded mozzarella cheese	Freshly ground black pepper

1. Preheat the oven to 375°F. Line a baking sheet with parchment paper and set aside.

2. Cut off a thin slice from the top of the tomatoes and discard. Carefully scoop out most of the pulp and discard it. The shell of the tomatoes should be about ½ inch thick. Salt the inside of the tomatoes and place them cut-side down on a paper towel to drain for 10 minutes.

3. Meanwhile, in a small bowl, stir together the bread crumbs, Parmesan and mozzarella cheeses, olive oil, and parsley. Season with pepper to taste. Stuff each tomato with several tablespoons of stuffing. Sprinkle additional Parmesan cheese on top. Place the tomatoes on the prepared baking sheet.

4. Bake for 30 minutes, or until the tops are browned. Serve hot.

Prep tip: The stuffing can be prepared several hours in advance, so feel free to prep it in the morning, refrigerate, and have it waiting when you get home from work!

PEAS WITH PROSCIUTTO AND SHALLOTS

Serves 4 to 6

Prep time: 10 minutes / **Cook time:** 25 minutes

5-Ingredient

Pass the peas, please! Peas are one of children's favorite vegetables in Italy. Although many kids shy away from anything green, give Italian kids peas with prosciutto and they will likely ask for seconds. Perhaps it has something to do with the added flavor from the prosciutto. This is a great side dish, but add 8 ounces of cooked shells or ditalini and you have a great first course.

3 tablespoons olive oil	8 slices prosciutto, chopped	2 cups water
2 shallots, chopped	1 pound frozen peas	Table salt

1. In a large sauté pan or skillet over medium-low heat, heat the olive oil. Add the shallots and cook for about 2 minutes until translucent. Add the prosciutto and cook for 3 to 4 minutes until crispy.

2. Add the peas and water and bring to a simmer. Cook, uncovered for about 15 minutes, or until the water evaporates. Taste for saltiness and season as needed; the prosciutto will add a lot of salt, so you may opt not to add any more. Transfer to a serving bowl and serve immediately while hot.

Substitution tip: This recipe is very adaptable. If you don't have shallots, use 1 small onion. No prosciutto? Use pancetta. Even the water can be swapped for low-sodium vegetable broth for more flavor.

PARMESAN BRUSSELS SPROUTS

Serves 4 to 6

Prep time: 10 minutes **/ Cook time:** 30 minutes

5-Ingredient

Brussels sprouts are a wonderful yet underutilized vegetable that make a great addition to any meal. They are part of the cabbage family and, like the larger counterparts, tasty in soups and vegetable stews. But one of my preferred preparations is roasted in the oven. The natural sugars caramelize and the Brussels sprouts practically burst with flavor in your mouth. Even if you've never been a fan, I think you'll agree these are delicious!

1 pound Brussels sprouts, stems trimmed, halved lengthwise

¾ cup freshly grated Parmesan cheese

¼ cup olive oil

¼ cup bread crumbs

½ teaspoon salt

Freshly ground black pepper

1. Preheat the oven to 375°F. Place an ungreased baking sheet in the oven to heat up.

2. In a large bowl, toss together the Brussels sprouts, Parmesan cheese, olive oil, bread crumbs, and salt to coat well. Season with pepper to taste. Carefully place the sprouts cut-side down on the hot baking sheet.

3. Roast for 15 minutes, flip the Brussels sprouts, and roast for 15 minutes more, or until fork-tender and crispy. Serve immediately while hot.

Substitution tip: Use this same method for cooking asparagus, which will cook in about half the time.

PAOLO MALDINI COCKTAIL

Serves 1

Prep time: 5 minutes

5-Ingredient / 30 Minutes or Less

I have a confession to make: I included this cocktail because it's named after one of my favorite Italian soccer players Paolo Maldini, who played for AC Milan. Besides that, this is an excellent drink! Refreshing and citrusy, it's the perfect accompaniment for any carb-loaded meal, such as pasta.

Table salt

Juice of 1 lime, lime reserved

1 ounce tequila

1 ounce Aperol

12 ounces grapefruit soda

Ice, for serving

1. Add enough salt to a shallow dish to coat the rim of your glass. Rub the lime over the rim of a 16-ounce glass. Dip the rim into the salt and shake off any excess.

2. Carefully add the tequila and Aperol to the glass and stir to mix.

3. Top with the lime juice and soda. Add ice and stir.

Pair it: Spaghetti alla Carbonara (page 43) is the classic combination to enjoy with this cocktail.

AMERICANO

Serves 1

Prep time: 5 minutes

5-Ingredient / 30 Minutes or Less

The Negroni (page 146) offers a nice strong tang, but when you need something a little lighter, go for the Americano. It offers a bit more of the Campari and vermouth but omits the strong gin and the alcohol is cut with the addition of club soda. It's so refreshing!

Ice, for serving

1½ ounces Campari

1½ ounces sweet vermouth

3 ounces club soda

Orange slices, for garnish (optional)

Fill a tall glass with ice. Add the Campari and sweet vermouth and mix well. Top with the club soda. Garnish with orange slices (if using).

> **Pair it:** The Americano is a nice *aperitivo* (opener) so enjoy it with the Arugula and Radicchio Salad (page 132) as a nice antipasto combination.

NEGRONI

Serves 1

Prep time: 5 minutes

5-Ingredient / 30 Minutes or Less

Nothing is as refreshing on a hot summer day as an ice-cold Negroni. It's a combination of bitter, sweet, and tangy. The vermouth offsets the bitterness of the Campari, and the color itself is enticing. It's a great apéritif while preparing your meal or as an accompaniment to any pasta. It can be shaken and poured into a glass, but I prefer it served over ice, which cuts some of the bitterness slightly.

Ice, for serving

1 ounce gin

1 ounce Campari

1 ounce sweet vermouth (preferably red)

Orange peel, for garnish (optional)

Fill a rocks glass with ice. Add the gin, Campari, and sweet vermouth. Stir well so all the ingredients are chilled. Top with an orange peel (if using).

Pair it: The Negroni is a perfect accompaniment to cheesy dishes, so enjoy with the Baked Italian Mac and Cheese (page 68).

APEROL SPRITZ

Serves 1

Prep time: 5 minutes

5-Ingredient / 30 Minutes or Less

The Aperol Spritz is perhaps one of the most recognized Italian drinks in the United States, thanks in part to a recent large US-based campaign from Campari, the maker of Aperol. Check out the hashtag #aperolspritz on Instagram just to see its popularity. The formula isn't complicated—3 parts bubbly wine (preferably prosecco), 2 parts Aperol, 1 part club soda. It's as easy as cocktails get, and it doesn't even require stirring—let the bubbles do the mixing for you!

Ice, for serving

3 ounces prosecco

2 ounces Aperol

1 ounce club soda

Orange slice, for serving

Add several ice cubes to your preferred glass. Pour in the prosecco. Add the Aperol, then the club soda. Drop in an orange slice and serve immediately so the ice doesn't dilute the drink.

Pair it: The Aperol Spritz is often served as an apéritif with a salty snack, so enjoy this drink with any recipe that calls for olives or anchovies.

MEASUREMENT CONVERSIONS

	US STANDARD	US STANDARD (OUNCES)	METRIC (APPROXIMATE)
VOLUME EQUIVALENTS (LIQUID)	2 tablespoons	1 fl. oz.	30 mL
	¼ cup	2 fl. oz.	60 mL
	½ cup	4 fl. oz.	120 mL
	1 cup	8 fl. oz.	240 mL
	1½ cups	12 fl. oz.	355 mL
	2 cups or 1 pint	16 fl. oz.	475 mL
	4 cups or 1 quart	32 fl. oz.	1 L
	1 gallon	128 fl. oz.	4 L
VOLUME EQUIVALENTS (DRY)	⅛ teaspoon		0.5 mL
	¼ teaspoon	———	1 mL
	½ teaspoon	———	2 mL
	¾ teaspoon	———	4 mL
	1 teaspoon	———	5 mL
	1 tablespoon	———	15 mL
	¼ cup	———	59 mL
	⅓ cup	———	79 mL
	½ cup	———	118 mL
	⅔ cup	———	156 mL
	¾ cup	———	177 mL
	1 cup	———	235 mL
	2 cups or 1 pint	———	475 mL
	3 cups	———	700 mL
	4 cups or 1 quart	———	1 L
	½ gallon	———	2 L
	1 gallon	———	4 L
WEIGHT EQUIVALENTS	½ ounce	———	15 g
	1 ounce	———	30 g
	2 ounces	———	60 g
	4 ounces	———	115 g
	8 ounces	———	225 g
	12 ounces	———	340 g
	16 ounces or 1 pound	———	455 g

	FAHRENHEIT (F)	CELSIUS (C) (APPROXIMATE)
OVEN TEMPERATURES	250°F	120°C
	300°F	150°C
	325°F	165°C
	350°F	180°C
	375°F	190°C
	400°F	200°C
	425°F	220°C
	450°F	230°C

RESOURCES

BOOKS

The 5-Ingredient Italian Cookbook by
    Francesca Montillo (Rockridge Press, 2018)
Back Pocket Pasta by Colu Henry (Clarkson Potter, 2017)
Everyday Pasta by Giada De Laurentiis (Clarkson Potter, 2007)
One-Pot Pasta by Sarah Walker Caron (Rockridge Press, 2019)
The Best Pasta Sauces by Micol Negrin (Ballantine Books, 2014)

BLOGS

Lazy Italian Culinary Adventures (theLazyItalian.com)
Italian Food Forever (ItalianFoodForever.com)
The Pasta Project (the-Pasta-Project.com)
Vincenzo's Plate (VincenzosPlate.com)

YOUTUBE

Laura in the Kitchen (youtube.com/user/LauraVitalesKitchen)
Natasha's Kitchen (youtube.com/user/NatashasKitchenBlog)
Pasta Grannies (youtube.com/user/PastaGrannies)

SHOPPING RESOURCES

I like Amazon for cooking equipment—they have everything!

For specialty Italian foods, the following sites are great resources:
Eataly.com
Gustiamo.com
ItalianFoodOnlineStore.com
SupermarketItaly.com

INDEX

ACKNOWLEDGMENTS

Much like my previous book, this book would have been impossible to write without the assistance and knowledge from the best culinary instructor I could ask for: my mom, Celeste. Everything I know about cooking comes from my mom, and to this day, when most people consult Google on how to do something, I consult Mom. Thank you for passing on all you know.

To my sister, Roseanne. My constant proofreader for everything that goes out! Thank you for your support and guidance during this process and in all I do.

To my dad, John, we shared countless pasta dishes together, but not nearly as many as I would have liked. I'll never have fettuccini without thinking of you.

And, as always, I wouldn't be able to do what I do without my beloved clients, both from my cooking classes and my Italian food and wine tours. Thank you for letting me share my culture with you.

Francesca Montillo is the author of *The 5-Ingredient Italian Cookbook: 101 Regional Classics Made Simple* (Rockridge Press, 2018). Francesca was born in Italy and currently divides her time between her native land and Boston, Massachusetts.

In 2016, Francesca combined her two passions, Italian food and travel, and started Lazy Italian Culinary Adventures (theLazyItalian.com). Combining the two things she loves most, she is now a culinary instructor and leads food and wine tours to Italy. Via her classes and team-building events in the Boston area, she is able to teach her students recipes that are uncomplicated, straightforward, and easily replicated at home.

Via her culinary adventures, Francesca is able to showcase the cuisine of her native country by bringing students and travelers to the source: Italy. On her tours, travelers partake in cooking classes with locals, visit honey and cheese farms, learn the olive oil-making process, and enjoy picnics at stunning vineyards. Francesca expertly designs all adventures, and some of her favorite destinations include the cities of Bologna, Florence, and Verona, as well as the southern regions of Calabria, Puglia, and Sicily.

Francesca is also a freelance food and travel writer, with work featured on *The Huffington Post, Tastes of Italia, Foodies of New England, Italian Sons and Daughters of America, Ambassador Magazine,* and several other notable outlets. Lazy Italian Culinary Adventures has been featured in *Forbes, The Boston Globe, Success Magazine, Wicked Local, Boston Voyager,* and *Medium,* to name just a few, as well as local TV shows. For information on her cooking classes or culinary adventures to Italy, you can visit her at theLazyItalian.com.

CPSIA information can be obtained
at www.ICGtesting.com
Printed in the USA
JSHW020320261020
8907JS00002B/5